MUSIC RIGHTS UNVEILED

Music Rights Unveiled provides an inside look at the complex world of music rights for film and video, and includes step-by-step guidance to navigate these tricky waters. Authors Brooke Wentz and Maryam Battaglia share their decades of expertise in this user-friendly guide, designed specifically with filmmakers and producers in mind. The book provides a brief history of the pricing of music in film, television and digital media markets, and explains the process by which music is licensed or acquired for films, highlighting pitfalls to avoid and strategies for success.

Further features include:

- A discussion of new media platforms and the intricacies of the rights needed to use music on those platforms;
- Tips for working with key music staff on a production – the composer, the music supervisor and the music editor;
- An in-depth explanation of building a budget for the music component of your media project.

Brooke Wentz founded The Rights Workshop, an established music licensing and supervision company, and more recently launched Seven Seas Music, a leading international music discovery platform. Former MD for ESPN, rights consultant to TechTV, and A&R manager for Arista Records, Brooke authored *Hey, That's My Music! Music Supervision, Licensing and Content Acquisition*. She spent years hosting various radio shows in NYC and won a Billboard Award for one of the best selling world music recordings. A graduate of Barnard College and Columbia Business School, she guest lectures and teaches around the world.

Maryam Battaglia's work combines her passion for music, media, and deal-making. She began her career in the music industry working at entertainment law firms with a focus on music publishing administration and licensing. Maryam later joined The Rights Workshop where she negotiates music rights on behalf of producers for film, television, online and emerging media. In 2015, she and Brooke co-founded Seven Seas Music. Maryam is a frequent speaker on music clearance and rights issues. She holds a B.A. from UCLA and a J.D. from California Western School of Law.

MUSIC RIGHTS UNVEILED

A FILMMAKER'S GUIDE TO MUSIC RIGHTS AND LICENSING

BROOKE WENTZ & MARYAM BATTAGLIA

NEW YORK AND LONDON

First published 2018
by Routledge
711 Third Avenue, New York, NY 10017

and by Routledge
2 Park Square, Milton Park, Abingdon, Oxon OX14 4RN

Routledge is an imprint of the Taylor & Francis Group, an informa business

© 2018 Taylor & Francis

The right of Brooke Wentz and Maryam Battaglia to be identified as the authors of this work has been asserted by them in accordance with sections 77 and 78 of the Copyright, Designs and Patents Act 1988.

All rights reserved. No part of this book may be reprinted or reproduced or utilised in any form or by any electronic, mechanical, or other means, now known or hereafter invented, including photocopying and recording, or in any information storage or retrieval system, without permission in writing from the publishers.

Trademark notice: Product or corporate names may be trademarks or registered trademarks, and are used only for identification and explanation without intent to infringe.

Library of Congress Cataloging in Publication Data
A catalog record for this book has been requested

ISBN: 978-1-138-67330-4 (hbk)
ISBN: 978-1-138-67331-1 (pbk)
ISBN: 978-1-315-56201-8 (ebk)

Typeset in Joanna MT Std
by Swales & Willis Ltd, Exeter, Devon, UK

For our daughters, Gabrielle and Olivia

CONTENTS

Foreword ix

1. Introduction: The Wild West, We Meet Again 1
2. The Law: For Those Respecting the Law, We Salute You. For the Rebels, There Is No Such Thing as Free Music 7
3. Background and History: When Synchs Outshine Soundtracks 33
4. Music Supervisors: Every Project Can Use a Little Music Supervision 47
5. Finding Music: A Community of Composers, Libraries and Representatives 61
6. The Process of Securing Rights: A Step-by-Step Guide to Avoiding Mistakes, Because What You Don't Know Can Cost You 87
7. Brand Personality, Identity and Recognition: People Rank Music as More Difficult to Live without than Sports, Movies and Newspapers 111

8. Digital Media and Digital Platforms: Welcome to the
   Digital Era in All Its Forms 125
9. For the Artist: There Is a Musician in All of Us 139
10. Conclusion: Parting Words of Encouragement 147

Glossary 151
Index 157

FOREWORD

Music Rights Unveiled is a much-needed guide to the role, use and licensing of music in practically any type of audio-visual production—whether it's a network, broadcast or cable television series, a major studio or independent film, a documentary or student film, an app, an advertising commercial, a webisode or a user-generated-content music video.

The authors, with their many years of experience in the field, break down and clearly explain every important aspect of how to use music in different types of productions, how one chooses the right music, how to make it work best to match the producer's vision and how to license it within prescribed budgets. Also covered are the basics of copyright as they apply to songs and sound recordings, the use of public-domain material, the difference between digital platform productions versus traditional media projects, the basic structure of a music license, price ranges for music licenses in various media and more.

A real bonus in the book is the best discussion I have ever seen in all my years of dealing in this area of the role and importance of music supervisors to any type of film, television or audio-visual production—from the development stage to pre-production to post-production to the final marketing of the finished product. They remain an essential part of the success of any production, large or small.

This book is written primarily for media producers-directors, producers, editors and music supervisors. But it is also valuable to anyone working in the field. It covers how you deal with the various types of music in film, television or any audio-visual work—the use of pre-existing songs and sound recordings, the considerations in choosing a composer to write an original score, the use and benefits of using pre-recorded and pre-cleared music from production music libraries and the benefits of hiring a music supervisor to handle all aspects of music in your production, both on the business side and the creative side.

Due to the increasing importance of audio-visual streaming services (Netflix, Amazon, Hulu, etc.) and social media sites (Facebook, YouTube, Instagram, Snapchat, Vimeo, etc.), music licensing and contracts have changed considerably in order to take into account these new digital platforms. These days the best music licenses cover as many distribution platforms as possible as you never know how and when consumers will be accessing your product. The authors cover Internet streaming rights in detail and explain the many options and considerations contained in these deals. In addition, they cover all of the non-Internet media rights, including film festival licenses, educational and art-house theatrical exhibition, non-theatrical and corporate use and the basics of traditional television licensing.

Todd Brabec, Esq., is a former ASCAP executive vice-president and worldwide director of membership. He is the co-author of *Music, Money and Success: The Insider's Guide to Making Money in the Music Business*, and is an adjunct professor at USC.

1

INTRODUCTION

The Wild West, We Meet Again

Almost every piece of visual media today—from user-generated YouTube videos to TV shows or films—has a musical component. Music helps move an image along and creates the emotional foundation for all visual content. It can make tears flow and tensions surge. Almost everyone we know loves music. Yet, ironically, when most producers or directors work on a film or media production, music is generally thought of toward the end of a project, during an edit or in post-production. Many times it tends to be the last money spent when resources begin to get scarce or eaten away by other line items. As a result, music doesn't always get the attention it deserves. But media creators who understand its importance relish the time when they can work with their chosen composer, or delve into their deep music catalogs, to pair the right vibe with an image.

One filmmaker made a documentary about a piano player who was blind, so after the edit and during post he put together a list of all the songs the protagonist had played in the film. With his list of songs, he needed to start getting permission from all the copyright holders. This process is called **clearance** or **copyright clearance**. However, because he could not gain permission from some of the copyright holders at a fee that he could afford, the songs had to come out of the production after he had locked picture. This is why it is important to think about your music sooner rather than later.

Another filmmaker spent years following Neil Diamond tribute bands around the country. After viewing the film, and to the surprise of the filmmaker, Mr. Diamond did not grant him permission to use his compositions, so the film had to be shelved.

A similar project about a Johnny Cash tribute band also had to be placed on hold, not because of song rights but because the Cash estate strictly prohibits projects involving tribute bands. Now, these may seem like dramatic examples, but they are real and you can't simply make a film about The Beatles and use Beatles songs without getting their blessing. It's just not going to happen.

Music rights, or permission to use the desired music, can be difficult to comprehend. There are complex terms and relationships that come with securing permission. On top of the practical issues, the news media continue to enjoy reporting on the next infringement case, the next non-payment stream to an artist and the downturn in music industry sales. The media highlights the cat-like predatorial stance that record labels and publishers take to sniff out infringers. This makes media creators apprehensive and diligent about wanting to obtain proper permission to use a piece of music. They wonder, can I use a particular song or not? Who do I ask for permission? Is it okay to use 10 seconds of a piece of music? It's on the Internet, so isn't it free?

No! It is not free or okay to use. But don't fret. That is why you are reading this book. We're here to help you through the labyrinth! To help unveil the myths and truths, and decipher the protocol required to secure what you need in order to make it work for you. Take a big breath. Sit back, relax and we'll walk you through it.

Music is an intangible asset. You can't hold it, cradle it, mail it, or even burn it. So when a media creator wants to incorporate a song into their production, a license must be obtained and the copyright owner must review the request and negotiate a fee. This is why mediators, or negotiators, exist. The easiest way to explain the granting of permission for the use of a song is to compare it to taking a book out of the library. You must return the book by a certain date, in the same condition. Similarly, when renting a car you have to have a driver's license, be a certain age and pay a certain price, and only then can you use the car for a select number of days, within a certain territory and for a specific fee. Licensing music is similar. You do not own the music. You are securing permission to use it in a specific **territory** for a specific **term**.

The most perplexing part about music rights is that the 'rental' fee varies based on territory, term (the number of days you want to use it), and where you want it to go, i.e., in which media. Pricing is subjective. What costs one client a particular fee may cost the next client double the fee, or half.

Adding to the complexity, the music licensing landscape has become more difficult due to the plethora of media as a result of the advent of digital technology. In the past, when a song's usage rights were being negotiated for a film, it would include traditional distribution forms such as film festival, theatrical, television, and home video. Now, there is also streaming, digital download, **video-on-demand**, Internet and Intranet, mobile/wireless and interactive, and the list goes on.

The protocol is time-consuming (it doesn't have to be), the paper trail is heavy (due to the legalities of copyright law), the search can be tiring (hunting out the appropriate copyright owners) and the back and forth of negotiation is complex (attention to detail is a must!). It's like walking a maze or solving a puzzle, so for those who like to speak this speak, the game can be exciting. There are a lot of pieces you have to put into place before you start the clearance work, and once they are in place the negotiating begins. You'll make a lot of twists and turns before you get to the end. But strike up the band, because the result can be a beautiful thing. There is nothing better than the most perfect song matching an image, and securing a fee within your budget.

Producers today walk a delicate line to obtain song usage rights, and unfortunately there is no 'blue book' to look up previous fees. It's the real Wild West of pricing: quotes for the use of music depend on what song it is, where it has been previously placed, whether the artist is 'recouped' or not (that is, is the artist's account with his record label in the red or black?), the song's market value, whether it is part of a premium catalog, where it is used in the production, whether there is a relationship between the director and composer, and numerous other variables. Trying to get a copyright owner to define a 'standard' price for something is almost impossible; no standard exists. The standard is what the buyer will bear and what the seller feels is the going price, dependent on previous fees. The music licensing process is based on protocol, and price depends on all the nuances of the particular circumstance of using that specific piece of music in that specific project. This is by no means easy to figure out, but this book will give you a toolbox of terms and strategies to negotiate your own deals and prepare you to speak intelligently to those who control the material you wish to use.

When a filmmaker seeks to obtain music clearance for their film, ad, TV show or new app, countless factors are considered. The most important item is media: the more exposure a piece of music has, the more it will cost. So with the advent of the Internet, where you can post a video on your Facebook page and someone across the world can see it, the media spread is large. This increased visibility is what copyright holders feel entitles them to charge more. You may say, "Wait a minute, only 200 people are seeing my video on the web! So I should not be charged as much." This is true. However, copyright holders assess the use based on *potential* reach, more than who will *actually* see it. This is exactly their job—to maximize the fee based on the media of exhibition. They reason it's how many potential eyeballs could see it, not how many actually see it.

In this book we will give you hints on how to navigate the maze, and hopefully show you where the land mines lie. Through our real-life examples and interviews with our lovely colleagues, we hope this book will help unveil the intricacies of music rights clearance and give you a deeper understanding of the process by which the **licensors** allow for copyright use.

We hope to demonstrate the ins and outs of music rights and music clearance, and give you a look into the role of a music supervisor as well. An equally important goal is to introduce you to the voice of the licensors, so that you get a good sense of their point of view and how their roles work. The best negotiators are those who understand both sides. We want to prepare you for these conversations and equip you with all the information that can help.

Together we have worked on over 500 projects in film, TV, advertising and new media. Our work at The Rights Workshop—a music supervision and clearance company—has been to finesse the delicate process of copyright clearance, and to secure the best prices for clients through understanding each detail of deal-making. We have had the opportunity to work on dozens of unique projects—lyrics on napkins, interactive karaoke machines, online instrument teaching games, virtual reality products, music in mobile sweepstakes, dancing flower-pots, and web-based talent shows. None is any stranger than another. We've written letters to artists in prison, sweet-talked lawyers who don't use email, wired money to Cairo on a Sunday and performed other unimaginable endeavors, all to get songs cleared in time and within budget. It's not easy. But it's crazy fun, and especially rewarding when projects come to fruition. Our stories make for great cocktail chit-chat and once you delve into this world, you will have plenty of your own! Enjoy.

—Brooke and Maryam

2

THE LAW

For Those Respecting the Law, We Salute You. For the Rebels, There Is No Such Thing as Free Music

If an artist of any sort—visual, music, film, written word—wants their work protected so that they can earn money from their art, it is highly recommended that they **copyright** the work. This is merely registering the art with the U.S. Copyright Office so that the artist is protected from future infringements, or, more simply, from anyone using their work. It's easy to register your work by going to www.copyright.gov. An application for copyright registration contains three essential elements: (1) a completed application form, (2) a non-refundable filing fee and (3) a non-returnable deposit—that is, a copy or copies of the work being registered and 'deposited' with the Copyright Office. When the Copyright Office issues a registration certificate, it assigns as the effective date of registration the date it received all required elements in acceptable form, regardless of how long it took to process the application and mail the certificate of registration.

Once your music or art is registered, you are then protected under U.S. **copyright law** from anyone using or incorporating parts or whole amounts of your work into theirs. Yet the proliferation of digital and social media platforms has rendered copyright law a mainstream issue with much considered debate. In today's world it is easier to poach someone's creative efforts, so much so that it has become relatively common. Copyright topics in the news vary widely from ownership disputes, extensions (the length of time a copyright is protected) and catalog valuations and acquisitions to infringement cases. Copyright law is the foundation of everything examined in this book. Without copyright protection, the creative endeavors of writers and producers would have no financial value. They would not be able to make a living. Therefore, the main reason one needs to clear or get permission to use music (the process of which is commonly called **music rights clearance**) is to secure a formal, legal **license** to use the music, because someone owns the underlying copyright and expects the **licensee** to recognize that and pay for that use.

While the breadth of copyright law is exhaustive and nuanced, the focus here will be on the purpose and basic principles that govern the issue. We'll discuss the historical origins, meaning and terminology behind commonly used phrases as well as the monetary value associated with copyright use.

PURPOSE

Copyright protection is instituted to encourage people to keep producing creative work for public consumption. Creative output is maximized when creators can be rest assured their blood, sweat and tears are respected and protected, and not stolen. Copyright is an acknowledgment of authorship and ownership. With protections in place, creatives can keep recording, writing and publishing with peace of mind.

From a user's perspective, copyright law serves an important role as well. Companies and media creators are able to use and incorporate the creation of others in their creative endeavors. More often than not, a producer comes to us having built his entire vision for a scene around the emotional elements of a piece of music. Creativity breeds creativity, so when an app developer is engineering a new game, or a filmmaker is envisioning a scene inspired by the work of another, the developer or filmmaker is able to incorporate that work into theirs and make something very special for their consumer and audience. Despite popular opinion, copyright law is not meant to hinder creativity. Quite the opposite; it's intended to inspire it.

HISTORY

Like most of our legal system, U.S. copyright law is based on British law. The idea originally was to protect people from the copying and reselling of published writings. In 1790, Congress enacted the first U.S. copyright statute, which was authorized by a clause in the Constitution that specifically protected **works of authorship**. This grew out of a need to protect the creators and writers of books, text and speeches, and orators. 'Works of authorship' expanded to include visual arts, motion pictures, photographs and songs. With the invention of the phonograph record, sound recordings were also included, and, most recently, digital content can be copyrighted. As of this publication, we live under the copyright framework established by the 1976 Copyright Act. This framework has been amended and the term of protection has been extended, but many principles of the Act remain the same.

DURATION OF COPYRIGHT

Determining the length of copyright protection has its complexities. For works created after 1978, the term of copyright is the life of the author plus 70 years. Works made for hire, which cover works created and owned by corporations, have a different standard: either 95 years from the date of publication or 120 years from the date of creation, whichever expires first. Whether protection extends to foreign infringers is another consideration. In 1887, the Berne Convention for the Protection of Literary and Artistic Works (named after Berne, Switzerland, where the Convention was signed), defined the scope of international copyright protection.

Under the terms of the Convention, reciprocal copyright protection was granted automatically to all creative works from member countries. It took the United States over 100 years to become a party to the Convention.

Figure 2.1 Berne Convention stamp, 1886

In 1989, the Convention established that an author is not required to register or otherwise apply for a copyright. As soon as the work is written or recorded, its author is automatically granted exclusive rights to the work until the copyright expires.

WHAT IS COPYRIGHTABLE AND WHAT ARE THE RIGHTS IT PROTECTS?

Protection under copyright law (title 17 of the U.S. Code, section 102) extends only to original works of authorship that are fixed in a tangible form. An 'original work' can be a book, a movie, a painting, a sculpture, songs, computer software and even architecture. 'Authors' or 'creators' can be writers, composers, visual artists, choreographers, filmmakers, architects, jewelry designers, musicians, and computer software programmers. They can be an individual, a corporation or a group of people. To be 'fixed' means it's been written down, recorded or notated on sheet music.

Now that we know what can be copyrighted, let's be clear on what cannot. Facts, ideas, systems or methods of operation are not copyrightable. Take a great tale of one man's efforts as a heli-medic in Aboriginal New Zealand. Great story? Yes. Copyrightable? No. You can't copyright a mere idea for a story. However, if the story is sufficiently 'original' you may be able to copyright the script.

Once an original work has been created and fixed, the copyright owner immediately acquires ownership of a number of important exclusive rights over that work. These unique rights include the right to reproduce, distribute, publicly perform, display publicly and make derivative works. Since these rights are owned and controlled by the copyright owner, any time a third party wishes to utilize one, the copyright owner must give permission, which is usually granted in the form of a license. A license is essentially an agreement, on paper, that states how, where, when and for what fee a user is allowed to use the piece of art or, in this case, music. Permission to use music copyrights has some commonly referred-to licenses. They are:

Mechanical License

This grants the user of music the right to reproduce a song in a physical or digital format via CD or digital download, provided the music has already been commercially released in the United States by the copyright owner. This is strictly for the audio reproduction of a song and does not pertain to any visual element that goes along with the audio. Let's say one wants to record and sell a cover album of hit sounds from one's high school years. A **mechanical license** would be required since the music is being performed in an audio-only format for release as a CD. Other examples include soundtrack albums and even karaoke use.

Public Performance License

This license grants permission for music to be heard in public spaces, such as on the radio or television, via on-hold music, or in an elevator, hair salon, local bar, or other places of work or even on a public website. This license is secured by public broadcasters, hence a radio station or television network, or a business establishment where music is heard. The licenses are generally granted on an annual basis, via a **blanket license**, so the venue has access to a ton of music, instead of licensing each song individually.

Synchronization License

This license grants permission to use a song which is locked to a moving image or other audio-visual body of work. This is the license that a filmmaker or media producer must secure when coupling images with music, since one is securing from the copyright owner the right to reproduction and distribution and the creation of a derivative work (i.e., the visual image which embodies the copyrighted material). Except for instances when a use is deemed 'fair' (which we will cover later in this chapter), almost every time a piece of music is paired with visual content a **synchronization license** has been secured through the copyright owner. Unlike the compulsory mechanical license or the blanket public performance license, a synchronization license needs to be negotiated almost every time.

MUSIC COPYRIGHT

Unfortunately, music copyright clearance is complex and unwieldy. The main reason being that, unlike other forms of art, there are at least two different entities to contact for clearance of a piece of recorded music. There is (1) the copyright holder of the recording and (2) the copyright owner of the underlying musical composition.

Why are there two copyrights? Well, because they are distinctively different. One protects the composition itself—which includes the music and lyrics—while the other protects a particular recorded version of that song. For example, let's consider the classic love song, "I Will Always Love You."

This song was written by Dolly Parton, and therefore she and her music **publisher**, Velvet Apple Music (BMI), own the copyright to the underlying musical composition. This song, however, has been recorded by dozens of artists, from Dolly Parton to LeAnn Rimes to Whitney Houston. Each of these recording artists, and their record labels, own the copyright in what is commonly referred to as the **master** of their particular recording of that song. This master copyright protects the sound recording and the creative efforts of the producer, sound engineers and background musicians. Therefore, when licensing the composition "I Will Always Love You" by

Figure 2.2 Dolly Parton cover "I Will Always Love You"—released 1974

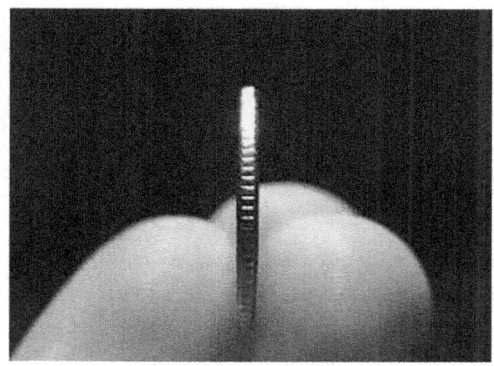

Figure 2.3 Two sides of a coin

Dolly Parton, it's important to understand both the label and the publisher need to grant permission. In industry jargon, this means both **sides** need to clear the song for your use. Think of a coin with two sides: (1) the master recording is one side, and (2) the composition, often referred to as the 'publishing,' is the other side.

Both 'sides' then must agree to the use before the requesting party can move ahead. This is the most important aspect of music rights clearance: 'one song, two rights.' Every song has two separate copyrights:

1. Publishing copyright—This covers the intellectual property concerning the creation of a piece of music, commonly known as 'songwriting credit.'
2. Master copyright—This covers the fixed audio record of a piece of music, including the performance and physical/digital recording of the song.

Although usually separate, there are some cases where the same entity controls both copyrights. More-independent companies such as Domino Music and Third Side Music usually sign an artist and then can represent both the publishing and master rights, or both 'sides.' When that happens the company is considered a **one-stop shop**, meaning that the user can obtain permission or clearance of both sides of the song at one company, rather than through a number of people. Music libraries such as Songtrdr and Pump Audio exist to do exactly that, i.e., be a one-stop for securing the music rights. Yet almost all popular commercial music will require a clearance from more than one entity.

FINDING THE COPYRIGHT OWNER

Copyright clearance can be tedious, in that owners are not always easy to locate or identify. As with any asset, rights switch hands. You can transfer and assign the right of a copyright at any time, so a copyright can be owned by one entity at the start of negotiations, and by the end controlled by a different entity, and hopefully not during the time of your project!

We worked with one client whose Oscar-nominated short had three songs in it that, when we initially cleared them, were affordable and cleared like butter. But then her film got greater distribution and we had to increase the rights she needed to cover all media. During the six-month lag period between the deals, the copyright holder for the famous song "New York New York," EMI, was sold to Sony/ATV Music. The new owners elevated this composition to being one of their premiere catalog songs, and the cost skyrocketed to more than four times the original fee. We spent months trying in any way possible to bring the price down to a more manageable fee. Over time we were successful in doing so. However, a change of ownership can wreak havoc on all parties.

Another common situation is when a new artist or songwriter holds the copyright personally and has not yet sold their rights to a publisher. A publisher's main role is to protect a copyright, exploit it and collect on the use of it. Most pay an up-front fee for a catalog of songs—previously recorded material or future songs—so they can control their use, instead of the songwriter overseeing the use of their music. They want the songwriter to focus on creating new material and leave the business aspects to the publisher.

To that end, a publisher and a label serve very similar core functions: chiefly, to earn money from the exploitation of their copyrights (a publisher on behalf of a song, and a label on behalf of a master recording). With revenue generation at the center of its business, a publisher is pressed to ensure all uses are properly licensed and therefore paid for. It's usually a lot easier to negotiate a deal with an unsigned songwriter/artist. For an indie, deal-making is motivated by many factors, not just money. Exposure for a band, genuine interest in a project and basic support for other creative communities still mean something. But this is often lost when publishers enter the picture. Publishers need to recoup the advance paid to control a catalog. They also need to make sure numbers are met to appease stakeholders. To be fair, some writers retain what is called an **approval right** over certain uses—usually synch uses—in which the agent, publisher or label representing the songwriter or artist must seek their content prior to licensing the music.

Once, our office cleared a Lorde song and the negotiated deal was handled through Lorde's management since she had yet to sign a publishing deal. By the time our client was ready to secure the license, the artist had inked a publishing deal with Songs Music Publishing, who then controlled the copyright to her music. Luckily for our client, this did not change the deal since the terms of use had been accepted and agreed to before she signed her publishing agreement. We were lucky in this case and timing was on our side.

The most laborious deal is when permission needs to be granted from a variety of copyright owners. This is common for certain types of music with multiple writers. For commercial music, obtaining permission from one party is not that common. There may be a variety of roads one must go down before determining the appropriate rights holders. A lot of hip-hop and Top 40 songs were written through collaboration between writers and producers. Beyoncé's "Run the World (Girl)" has 6 writers and 7 publishers, while "Power" by Kanye West boasts a ridiculous 14 writers and 8 publishers. Needless to say, when a client comes to us wishing to license one of these titles, we politely advise them against it because there are simply too many entities from which approval must be sought. Or we ask them to be patient and ditch the deadline, as it will take time and patience to get the music fully cleared.

For the Netflix original series *Last Chance U* we cleared the Young Thug song "Best Friend" through his lawyer. The lawyer only represented 40% of the song, but after five months of negotiation in which a license was issued and revised to suit their needs, the lawyer for Young Thug informed us that two publishers had purchased the rights, and so we had to start from scratch to secure them.

COPYRIGHT SPLITS

Splits or **copyright splits** involve ownership percentages. Since there can be multiple writers, there can be splits in the copyright shares. A composition's ownership must add up to a total of 100% worldwide interest in and to a copyright. If a songwriter is part of a group of writers, it is important to confirm clearance of the entire song. Many songwriters enjoy the process of writing but may not understand, or feel comfortable, drawing a line between business and pleasure. When two musicians get together for a session and one writer says, "Hey man. It was great to play with you, let's do this again," hopefully they come to an agreement as to what percentage of the song each holds. If this is not sorted out, the song could be left registered to the wrong entity or with incorrect splits, and any future earnings will go to the wrong entity.

Likewise, it is essential for any person wanting to use a song that in order to incorporate the composition into a production, all the contributing writers of the song must be contacted to secure approvals. This ensures that 100% of a song is cleared for use. If there are two people who wrote a song, generally the split is 50/50. For example, Ed Sheeran's song "Thinking Out Loud" was written by Edward Christopher Sheeran and Amy Wadge. The writers' share is split 50/50 between the two, whereas the song "The A Team" was written solely by Ed, hence he controls 100% of this song.

Thinking Out Loud	Edward Christopher Sheeran (PRS)	Sony/ATV Music UK (PRS)	50%
	Amy Victoria Wadge (PRS)	BDI Music c/o Roynet Music (PRS)	50%

The A Team	Edward Christopher Sheeran (PRS)	Sony/ATV Music (BMI)	100%

So, in this case, if you wanted to use "Thinking Out Loud" you would have to obtain permission from the two writers via their publishers, Sony/ATV and BDI. In many electronic dance tracks there are multiple writers. Take, for example, Jack Ü, the collaboration between Skrillex and Diplo, and their song "Where Are Ü Now," featuring Justin Bieber.

Where Are Ü Now	S. Moore (ASCAP), J. Ware (BMI)	Kobalt (BMI)	23%
	K. Brutus (BMI)	BMG (BMI)	27%
	T. Pentz, Pooh Bear (Jason Boyd) (ASCAP)	Songs (BMI)	20%
	J. Bieber (ASCAP)	Universal (ASCAP)	30%

Or "How Deep Is Your Love" by Calvin Harris and Disciples:

How Deep Is Your Love	Gavin Koolmon (PRS), Luke McDermott (PRS), Adam Richard Wiles (ASCAP)	EMI (PRS), Fly Eye Publishing Ltd, Phrased Differently Music Ltd (PRS), TSJ Merlyn Licensing BV—ALL EMI	53.34%
	Nathan Vincent Duvall (BMI)	BMG (BMI)	16.6%
	Christine Ina Wroldsen (PRS)	Reservoir 416 (BMI)	30%

Although uncommon, one may encounter what is called a **split dispute** wherein the total ownership value in and to a composition adds up to less than or greater than 100%. This information is usually discovered during the clearance process, when the copyright owners tell you what their percentage shares are. Split disputes pose a challenge in that they may cause a delay in getting a piece of music clearance. The copyright owners will check with their copyright departments to check the contracts governing the music. They may reach out to each other to discuss the matter. This can all result in delays in getting the piece cleared or, worse, deem the music un-licensable until the dispute is resolved. We saw this issue when clearing the Gene Vincent song "Be-Bop-A-Lula" for a live performance. The song was cleared for $2,500. There were three copyright holders—Warner Chappell, Sony/ATV, and Music Sales—and the following ownership percentages were given at the time of the production:

Song Title	Publisher	Fee
Bee-Bop-A-Lula	Sony/ATV (83.33% USA & 100% of Canada) = 42.50% World	$1,062.50
	Three Wise Boys Music c/o Embassy c/o Music Sales (16.67% of USA and 16.67% of BRTs) = 11.68% World	$292.00
	WC (100% of World excluding USA and Canada) = 50% World	$1,250.00
Total		$2,604.50

As you can see, the numbers total more than the agreed fee, so the dispute was discussed and months later rectified. However, note that a dispute is not always about percentages, but can involve territories of ownership as well.

INFRINGEMENT OF COPYRIGHT

Copyright infringement occurs when someone violates the exclusive rights of the copyright owner, or, essentially, uses the song without permission. Whether or not a song is actually registered with the U.S. Copyright Office, the copyright owner's work is protected. We have heard this question many times: "I looked up the song and it was not registered. So it's free to use, right?" Wrong. A work is copyrighted the second it is fixed in any tangible medium. One would have to attempt to find the songwriter. Registration is not a precondition to copyright protection; it's a formality that most importantly establishes that the certain work was in one's possession at a specific time. Some folks like the old **poor man's copyright** method. Say, for whatever reason, you do not wish to register your work. Instead, you place the song in an envelope and mail it to yourself. When it's returned to you it has your name and a date stamp to positively prove that the work at least belonged to you as of the date on the stamp. The problem is, there is nothing in the law that acknowledges the validity or accuracy of this method. When you formerly register a song with the Copyright Office you fill out an online form, pay the registration fee, lay out your copyright, and if the registration is accepted your copyright is said to be registered. So why not do it? Registration establishes a public record of the copyright claim and makes it easier to bring a law suit against an infringer. Certain remedies are available when a work has been physically registered versus when it has not. For example, in general cases of infringement due to naïveté or ignorance, liability for civil copyright infringement involves actual damages and profits, which can be very difficult to prove. If the work has been registered, however, **statutory damages** range from $750 to $30,000 per work infringed, and up to $150,000 per work infringed if it can be proved that the plaintiff willfully (or knowingly) infringed. Statutory damages are awards set by the court because it cannot be determined what the copyright owners' actual losses were or what the plaintiffs' actual gains were. A court also has the discretion to assess costs and attorneys' fees too, which is among the greatest inducements to registering a work.

It is important to note that each owner of each exclusive right may have a claim against an infringer. This is because any exclusive right (i.e., the right of reproduction, the right to make a derivative work or the right to publicly perform a work) may be assigned or licensed to a third party, or multiple third parties. For example, most publishers utilize the Harry Fox Agency to handle mechanical licensing on their behalf, or ASCAP, BMI and SESAC to handle public performance licensing on their behalf. The individual publisher handles everything else. So, for example, if a filmmaker released a film without securing a synchronization license and in addition released a soundtrack album containing that song without securing a mechanical license, both the publisher and Harry Fox would have separate claims as each of their exclusive rights were violated by unlicensed use.

Filmmakers always ask, "Will I get sued if I use this song?" No. Practically speaking, a filmmaker using a song that has not been cleared (or for which permission has not been obtained) for use in their production will rarely, if ever, go to court. What will occur, however, is that they will receive a lovely formal **cease-and-desist** letter from a lawyer which puts an infringer on notice prior to any action. This notice usually contains a demand that an action be taken (e.g., remove the music from future sales units of the film, or remove the film from a website or third-party streaming platform). Here's an example of such a letter:

To Whom It May Concern,

This firm represents the recording artist professionally known as Superior Dogsleds ('Artist'). It has come to our attention that www.operatingwithoutlicense.com ('Website') is currently selling and otherwise exploiting audio-visual music lessons via the Internet which embody musical compositions written and controlled by Artist ('Compositions').

Please be advised that our client has not granted to Website or any other individual or entity on Website's behalf any rights whatsoever to exploit or otherwise use the Compositions. Website's actions constitute, among other things, infringement of our client's copyrights therein.

Based on the foregoing, we hereby demand, on behalf of our client, that you immediately remove any audio or audio-visual lesson, and other materials which embody the Compositions, from the Website (and any and all associated URLs) and cease and desist from any further exploitation or other use of the Compositions. Demand is further made that you immediately account to us for any and all revenues you have received in connection with your use of the Compositions, from the date of first exploitation until present date. We also demand that you provide us with any and all information available with respect to sales or other exploitations of the Compositions. Please notify us that you intend to comply with the foregoing demands.

If you fail to comply with the aforesaid demands within ten (10) days from the date hereof, then please be advised that our client has authorized us to take any and all action necessary or appropriate in the circumstances to vigorously enforce our client's rights and remedies at law and equity. Without limiting the foregoing to the extent you have knowledge of the facts set forth herein and continue to exploit the Compositions, we intend to seek any and all punitive damages available as a result of your actions in bad faith in connection with this matter.

All rights reserved.

Sincerely,
Counsel for Artist

Basically, the infringer is told to stop infringing, pay a penalty for the infringed use (based on prior exploitation of the production) or negotiate a fee to move forward and continue using the music. In our experience, which deals in the use of music in synchronization with a film or other audio-visual production, we have yet to see any copyright use of a song go to court. In film, especially in independent films, having the infringer stop (rather than pay up) is more important. The infringer would almost always be asked to correct the infringement on further distributions of the film, so that if they haven't released it on DVD yet, they must correct the DVD. If a fee is required, it is usually established by calculating how many exhibitions of the film or project have taken place and the market value is paid. Far more sticky are the court cases involving infringements where substantial amounts of money are involved. These suits pertain to copyright infringement when an infringement involves use of music in a new, commercially released track, such as the Marvin Gaye/Robin Thicke case for "Blurred Lines," or The Verve's "Bittersweet Symphony," which integrates five notes of the Rolling Stones' "The Last Time." In the "Blurred Lines" case, the song was tremendously popular at the time, so winning in court would be a windfall for the estate, which indeed it was.

There are also Name and Likeness cases: for example, in the Tom Waits vs. Frito-Lay case, the client Frito-Lay did not secure the rights to Mr. Waits' recording of "Step Right Up." Instead it found a singer who sounded exactly like Tom Waits, and used their recording of the song. Since the recording sounded so similar to the original, the client stepped on Mr. Waits' signature vocal style and hence this was ground for infringement. Mr. Waits won the 1992 case.

Although not required by law, if there is a copyright notice on any type of work that is planned to be used in your production, pay attention and make sure to license it. There is the copyright in the composition, marked with a © symbol, and copyright for publicly distributed records, etc., with the symbol ℗. The ℗ refers to the year of the first publication of the sound recording, while © refers to the owner of the composition. Both symbols are accompanied by the names of the owners of the copyright, i.e., the songwriters (or the music publisher) and the artist (or the label).

FAIR USE DEFENSE

It has been mentioned that copyright infringement occurs whenever someone violates the exclusive rights of a copyright owner, with some limitations or exemptions. **Fair use** is one such exemption. Fair use is a legal doctrine that allows anyone (under Section 102 of the Copyright Act) to copy, publish, or distribute parts of a copyrighted work, without permission, in limited circumstances: as commentary, news reporting or parody or as scholarly work. Fair use is a concept that is frequently debated and frequently misunderstood. Section 107 of the Copyright Act sets out the four factors that may be used in determining whether a filmmaker may claim fair use as a defense to copyright infringement:

- purpose and character of the use;
- nature of the copyrighted work;
- amount and substantiality of the portion used in relation to the copyrighted work as a whole;
- effect of the use upon the potential market for or value of the copyrighted work.

Courts will look at the amount of material used and whether the unlicensed use 'transforms' or adds value to the material taken from the copyrighted work. However, the reality is that there is no black and white rule to determine whether a use is fair or qualifies as a parody.

A use is not deemed 'fair' until a court says it is, so guidance in this area rests heavily in case law. Content users will often license the copyright in question in order to avoid unpleasant legal consequences or litigation. But before succumbing, it is strongly recommended to seek legal counsel and obtain an opinion. There are strong advantages to seeking legal review of your film for fair-use assessment. Some are dissuaded given the cost in 'lawyering up,' yet it is usually a big cost saving should a review reveal that many items do not need to be licensed. **Opinion letters** are letters written by lawyers. They render legal opinion on whether or not certain assets used in your film could be used pursuant to fair use. They are great to have on file should you need to provide one to an insurance company as part of an errors and commissions package, or to the film distributor.

"Case law is extremely strong on the fair use points, especially in documentaries," says Lisa Callif of Donaldson and Callif, LLP, an entertainment law firm which specializes in the representation of independent producers in film, television and web-based content.

> In features there's not as much case law going on. But still, all the people out there really support a storyteller's right to use a limited amount of information for the purpose of comment or criticism. And whatever that may be—whether a studio film or a photograph or a piece of music—the same rules apply across the different types of intellectual property. This is why we can do what we do [write opinion letters] and insurance companies will accept them.

Donaldson and Callif work on numerous films a year. They have identified a pattern that can help filmmakers confidently determine whether the use of copyrighted material in their film could be deemed fair use; that is, if, for a non-fiction project, they can answer affirmatively to these three questions:

1. Does the asset illustrate or support a point that the creator is trying to make in the new work?
2. Does the creator of the new work use only as much of the asset as is reasonably appropriate to illustrate or support the point being made?
3. Is the connection between the point being made and the asset being used to illustrate or support the point clear to the average viewer?

Seeking the advice of counsel early on is also better from a budgetary standpoint. The cost to hire a lawyer to review your film and provide a fair-use assessment will be much less than the cost to license all the music and clips being used. Additionally, when you do not enter into a license agreement, it follows that you will not be responsible to pay reuse fees. This responsibility is passed on to filmmakers from the producers as part of the standard language contained in the license agreements. Filmmakers save money by not only avoiding payment of a license fee, but they also avoid the obligation of paying union reuse fees. Unions like the American Federation of Musicians and the American Federation of Television and Radio Artists collect payments for the reuse of recordings in motion picture as if the musician who rendered services for the sound recording walked onto set and rendered services for the use of that recording in the film. These payments are charged to the licensors, who pass the obligation on to the filmmaker in their synch licenses.

Lisa Callif says,

> We can help filmmakers formulate how they are going to move forward. We assess what will license and what won't. We work with them so that the client can properly license what they need to license, and properly fair-use what they need to fair-use. When a client comes later seeking an opinion it becomes more tricky. There is still time to fair-use things but it doesn't change the legal arguments. It can put you on the radar of that licensor and create an uncomfortable situation. This of course incurs legal fees since lawyers have to go back and negotiate things for a nominal fee through what's sometimes referred to as a 'fair use' license.

FAIR USE IN ADVERTISING

When something is used pursuant to fair use in the body of a film, it does not mean that the same material could be used out of context in a promo for the film. In fact, it almost never can. Promo use raises several other issues, such as publicity rights, that are not relevant when the use of the material, for example, was circumstantial in the body of the film. Promos or trailers are seen as marketing tools. "With promos, the music is taken out of context and therefore is no longer fair use," says Callif.

For example, our firm worked on the documentary film *Glen Campbell: I'll Be Me*.

In the film, some clips were used pursuant to fair use. When it came time to release a series of promo spots for the film, the team had to remove these clips because they were being used out of context. Just because something is fair game in the film does not mean it is fair game for use in a trailer. Its purpose is to advertise rather than add commentary, much like the documentary itself.

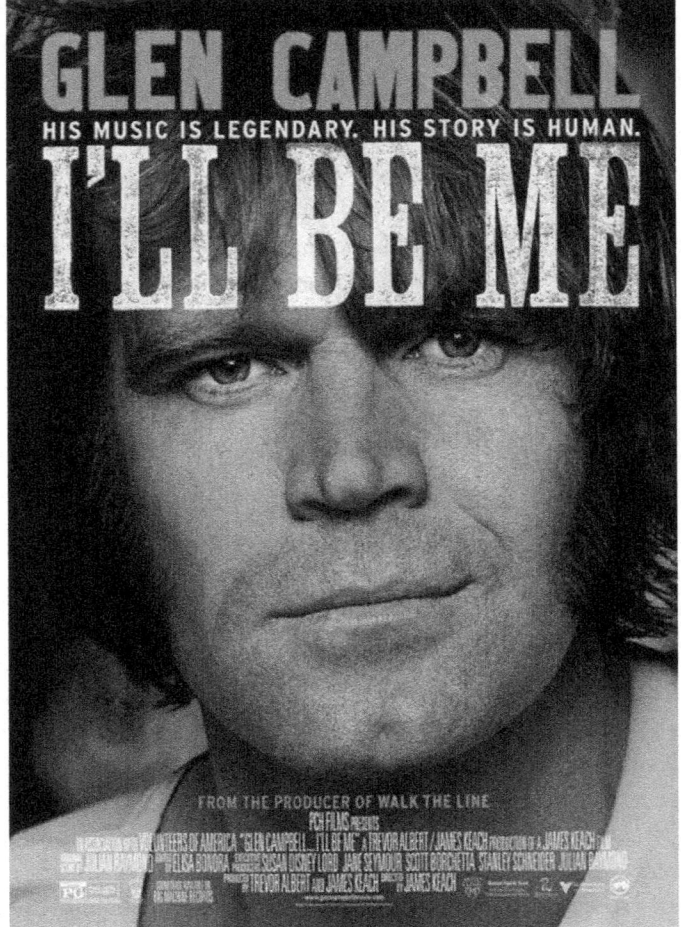

Figure 2.4 Glen Campbell: I'll Be Me—2014

CREDITS IN FAIR USE

So if something is being used 'fairly' and therefore does not require a license, should one still credit the song in the end credits, or list the use in the **cue sheet**? A cue sheet is a log document that lists all the compositions in the body of a film or television production. It is a delivery requirement of all public broadcasters and exhibitors in order to compensate songwriters for the public performance of their music. (See Chapter 6 for a detailed look at cue sheets.)

Not licensing the material is declaring that there is no need to secure a license for the use of the music in a film, but adding the music on the cue sheet would still afford the writers performance income, which is a responsibility of the broadcasting entities, not the filmmaker. Whatever position you take, or are advised to take by your lawyer, we would recommend not to credit the fair-used material in the same way the licensed material is credited. Material used pursuant to fair use has its own credit section, such as 'Additional music' or 'Additional footage.'

Fair use is by no means all or nothing. If you decide to fair-use portions of your film, it doesn't mean you won't be doing any licensing. Many times a project includes both, and this is when a clear understanding between the production's legal counsel and the clearance person is important. The objective is to have a fully cleared film at the end of the day, and therefore the job of the clearance person is to deliver all copyrighted materials as designated by the chosen legal counsel. Having a skilled team beside you will make the process move as smoothly and effectively as possible.

PUBLIC DOMAIN

Copyright protection does not last forever. When copyrighted works expire (dependent on what year the work was created) they fall into what is called the **public domain**. A work is in the public domain when no one can find any law that gives them legal claim to that property. When a piece of music is in the public domain, it is considered communal property and can be used freely without permission and in any way one can imagine. You can arrange, reproduce, perform, record or publish it, and use or sell it commercially.

A popular rule of thumb is that all works created prior to 1923 are in the public domain. Some examples are traditional, religious and classical music. As with all rules, however, there are exceptions. This general rule does not

Figure 2.5 Public domain song "Jingle Bells"—1857

address unpublished works, extensions, and a variety of other exemptions. It also does not address arrangements of public-domain work, which may be copyrighted even if the original work falls in the public domain. A good example of this is the song "Jingle Bells," which was originally written by James Lord Pierpont in 1857.

The original song is in the public domain. However, there are dozens of versions of "Jingle Bells," so you need to check whether the arrangement you decide to use is copyrighted. When a public-domain song has been rearranged, the new arrangement can by copyrighted and protected under U.S. copyright law. One example is the popular Christmas rock version, "Jingle Bells Rock" by Bobby Helms. This is a fun, upbeat version of the popular tune and a standard on Christmas compilations. Or there is the Brian Setzer Orchestra's published arranged version that replaces "one-horse open sleigh" in the first verse with "'57 Chevrolet." Together these new lyrics and its big-band feel make the song a classic licensing favorite for special products and contemporary film scenes. This is just one example of many where it is important to do some digging when using a seemingly public-domain song in your film. If you include the song with the mistaken assumption that it is in the public domain, the copyright holder has grounds to sue, or issue a cease-and-desist, because the work you decided to use was under copyright protection. Always check whether the particular arrangement of a public-domain work that you want to incorporate into your production is copyrighted. You can do so by checking first at www.pdinfo.com or paying an outside service such as the Motion Picture Information Service (MPIS), owned and operated by Elias Savada, to do the research for you and provide documentation to back up your claim.

Here is an example of a public-domain search report provided by MPIS for the song "Mary, Don't You Weep":

- -

Mary, Don't You Weep No registration and/or renewal was found for the published music of the arrangement by Inez Andrews [1929–2012] of this 1958 hit song for which she sang lead for The Caravans. The tune, alternately titled **O Mary Don't You Weep, Oh Mary, Don't You Weep, Don't You Mourn**, and other variations is a Negro spiritual that originated from before the American Civil War. It was first recorded in 1915. A performance of the song was included on the sound recording **The Remarkable Inez Andrews with the True Voices of Christ Concert Ensemble, Recorded 'Live' in Chicago, Illinois—SL 14591**. It was registered for copyright SF-22-408 on November 21, 1980 by Savoy Records, Inc. (PO Box 279, Elizabeth NJ 07207), citing 1980 as the year of creation and November 12, 1980 as the date of publication in the United States. The 33 1/3rpm disc was distributed by Arista Records.

- -

THE INTERNET

The Internet has also introduced a slew of new issues because now people can make money from videos. Some rights holders may immediately request the blocking of a video that contains unlicensed copyrighted songs. Others may let it slide, either because subjectively they like the video, or because the video has received 1 million views in an hour and the rights holders will be monetizing on the back end. This means that in some cases an uploaded video featuring, for example, a kitten dancing to Katy Perry's "Roar" will not be blocked since the video has received millions of views and the rights holders are generating money or 'monetizing' the video via ads that are running on the site, which is the case on YouTube.

If you do receive a notice to remove your video, here is what it may look like. Don't panic. It's just a notice, not a lawsuit. Address the notice and correct the matter and all will be well.

- -

We have received a formal DMCA (Digital Millennium Copyright Act) notice regarding allegedly infringing content hosted on your site. The specific content in question is as follows:

www.operatingwithoutlicense.com

The party making the complaint,

John Smith
The Company
111 Fair Street
Burbank, CA 91505

claims under penalty of perjury to be or represent the copyright owner of this content. Pursuant to 17 U.S.C. § 512(c), we have removed access to the content in question.

www.loc.gov/copyright/title17/92chap5.html#512

If you believe that these works belong to you and that the copyright ownership claims of this party are false, you may file a DMCA counter-notification in the form described by the DMCA, asking that the content in question be reinstated. Unless we receive notice from the complaining party that a lawsuit has been filed to restrain you from posting the content, we will reinstate the content in question within 10–14 days after receiving your counter-notification (which will also be forwarded on to the party making the complaint).

In the meantime, we ask that you do not replace the content in question, or in any other way distribute it in conjunction with our services.

Please also be advised that copyright violation is strictly against our Terms and Conditions, and such offenses risk resulting in immediate disablement of your account should you not cooperate (not to mention the legal risk to you if they are true).

We also ask that if you are indeed infringing upon the copyright associated with these works that you delete them from your account immediately, and let us know once this has been done. We also ask that you delete any other infringing works not listed in this takedown notification, if they exist.

If you have any questions, please don't hesitate to let us know.

Regards,

Copyright law is extensive and multifaceted. It produces unending legal, ethical, and intellectual discourse. There are various ways that a creative and business affairs professional might consider to evaluate a piece of content. The issue keeps everyone busy—lawyers, publishers, labels, managers and, of course, music supervisors and clearance companies. In the end, artists need to be compensated in order to continue creating valuable works, and their work needs to be respected and acknowledged. In order to protect themselves from misuse they must register their works, and it is the artist's right to withhold or extend the privilege to the use of their property. It's important to always imagine yourself on the other side of the fence. This is key in negotiating, and once respect and mutual consideration are achieved, licensors and content users will be able to work together in greater harmony, a key component in a truly rich, creative society.

3

BACKGROUND AND HISTORY

When Synchs Outshine Soundtracks

Music is a complex copyright to understand mainly because there are two copyright holders in a piece of recorded music. There is the copyright in the composition, which is controlled by the publisher; and the copyright in the recording, which is generally held by the record label or, if not, a company that commercially released the recording.

A publisher oversees the use and exploitation of copyrights. This could be a handful of songs held by one individual, or thousands of songs and catalogs held by a major company like Universal Music Publishing or Sony/ATV Music Publishing. Any use of their copyrights via sale through recording or print publication, or the use of a composition synchronized in any media production, such as a film, TV show, advertisement, video game or webisode, allows income to be earned by the writer. For example, when a song is re-recorded by an artist, the songwriter receives a mechanical royalty derived from the mechanical license for each sale of the recording. An example is when Panic! At the Disco covered Queen's "Bohemian Rhapsody." Each time the song is downloaded and purchased the original writer of "Bohemian Rhapsody," Freddie Mercury, receives a mechanical fee (currently set by U.S. rate courts at $0.091 for a song running up to five minutes) for each purchase. When the song is used in a film, or synchronized, as it was in the motion picture *Suicide Squad*, a synchronization use fee is provided by the publisher for its use.

On the other hand, a record label that controls the other copyright in a commercial piece of music provides a similar function, i.e., overseeing the exploitation of the recording. However, this is not its main duty. The primary activity of a record label is to produce and sell recorded music. It finds talent, signs artists to a contract (also known as a record deal), and in return gives the artist money to produce a recording, and a royalty rate based on sales. The label then markets the artist, via music videos, radio play, touring and advertisements, in order to gain sales. This is, and has been, the primary source of income for labels, whether the music was sold on vinyl or tape, or via digital download and now streaming.

Yet one big difference between a publisher and a label is that publishers have been doing their same job—protecting and exploiting compositions—for years and years. Record labels have been around for a shorter time and their primary purpose is to sell music. Only over the last 30 to 40 years has licensing (the permission by one company to allow another company use of its assets) become a very important income stream to labels. The internal term for the exploitation of a recording is called **third-party licensing** and this pertains to any money received by a label that is not generated by selling music. It is sometimes referred to as **ancillary income**—income generated by a company for services outside its core business or primary product offering. Examples are revenue generated by licensing music for compilation albums, synchronization and artist marketing endorsements. A film soundtrack album, for example, would be a third-party license where many different songs are compiled together for a new release. These songs generally come from various artists on different record labels.

With the advent of single-song streaming, however, **compilation albums** (the assembly of a variety of songs from various sources to create one album) have been on the decline. They are more relevant when a soundtrack is needed for a film or TV producer. What has exploded is the rapid increase of income in the area of **master use licensing** (the licensing of a master or particular recording into moving media). This is when music is locked with a picture or image via film, TV, games, ads or webcasting and is heard in time with it.

In the past, record labels would have one or two people hired to work in the area of third-party licensing. However, over the years, due to the plethora of music used in various media productions, those departments have grown to twenty persons or more due to mounting requests for music in film and TV.

Synchronization use, formerly considered an insignificant revenue stream to the labels, has ballooned into very important income for both publishers and record labels. In the past, when a record was made, the main source of income for both the publisher and the label was through retail sales. Today is vastly different.

Bob Fukuyama, Senior Director, Film and TV Licensing, at the Warner Music Group, has been involved in synchronization licensing for over three decades. He was hired by Warner Special Products (WSP) to help launch the first dedicated synch licensing department in the record business. WSP had taken over all synch licensing responsibilities on behalf of the Warner family of record labels at the beginning of 1983. Up to then, the core Warner labels—Warner Bros., Elektra, Atlantic—had shown minimal interest in developing synchronization licensing as a business or as a profit center.

Bob Fukuyama was brought on board by Mark Leviton, Vice-President of WSP, in the 1980s. This division was originally founded in 1973 by Mickey Kapp, with the mission to handle all ancillary markets—i.e., everything outside of regular retail—on behalf of the Warner family of record labels. While WSP's mission included all third-party licensing, it did not include synch at the outset, as there was no viable synch business at the time.

As Fukuyama recounts,

> Warner Special Products was modeled after the granddaddy of all Special Products divisions, Columbia Special Products, who had been the undisputed market leader for decades. Columbia was the biggest American record company at that time, and they not only dominated the Special Products space for decades, but they had the largest record club.

Figure 3.1 Andy Williams—Columbia record club—1971

Record clubs were a monthly subscription service that sent subscribers new record releases each month. They made a fortune selling records by getting subscribers via TV ads, much like Home Shopping Network today. In the 1970s, music was sold only in record stores, so to receive a selection of new releases each month via mail by subscribing to a record club, such as Columbia or K-Tel International, was a luxury.

"K-Tel helped define the TV-advertised hits compilation market," continues Fukuyama,

> [t]heir 'Hits' compilations were hugely successful, often selling several million units, and provided a steady stream of licensing income to the labels, often with substantial advances. Because the TV spots were so aggressive, they helped hammer home the names of artists to consumers who may not have heard of them. Regarding front-line artists, at WSP we were able to show the labels that our K-Tel licensing deals did not cannibalize from sales of the artist's own albums, as our market research revealed that K-Tel buyers represented their own market niche.

Mickey Kapp, President of WSP, was the first record executive to identify synchronization licensing as a potentially lucrative, and important, business for record companies. He saw it as a growth area on the brink of exploding, given that the baby boom generation was taking over the creative content (and management) of the film and television industries.

"His father David Kapp started an independent label called Kapp Records in New York City," recounts Fukuyama,

> [t]hey had a smash hit with Brian Hyland's "Itsy Bitsy Teenie Weenie Yellow Polkadot Bikini" in 1960. Ironically, in light of Mickey's involvement with synch later, the song was prominently featured in Billy Wilder's 1961 Berlin Wall comedy, *One, Two, Three*, when the East German secret police tortured a suspected spy by playing the record repeatedly.

After learning the record business at Kapp, Mickey moved to Los Angeles, where he held executive positions at Capitol and then Elektra. At Elektra, he pitched the Warner labels on the idea of a Special Products division based on the successful Columbia Special Products model, and, in 1973, WSP opened for business.

> These were the years when the record business exploded and expanded rapidly, so Mickey's timing was perfect: the labels were so busy signing and developing artists and selling records at the thousands of record stores and other retail outlets across the country that they had no time and no interest in developing ancillary markets for their assets. If anything, the labels were thrilled to be able to hand over the responsibility for these low-money and unsexy areas—which they often considered an annoyance—to Warner Special Products.

While Kapp sold the idea of WSP mainly as a service entity—serving the labels by undertaking sole responsibility for areas that they considered a very low priority—he also saw WSP as a profit center not completely dependent on the success of the Warner labels; his ambition was to aggressively grow the business in each of the traditional Special Products categories, i.e., manufacturing custom products and custom series for TV marketers and direct-mail marketers, and licensing to third parties. WSP was very successful throughout the 1970s and 1980s, not only by working with the K-Tels, but also by compiling their own TV-advertised albums: in order to create products with maximum sales potential, WSP would license in tracks from outside record companies to supplement the tracks from the Warner catalog; a 50-track WSP TV-advertised album would usually contain 35–40 tracks licensed in from outside record companies. (In addition to compiling these albums, WSP would handle the manufacturing, and in the end delivered the finished goods to the TV and direct-mail marketers, who would fulfill the orders.) But in identifying synch licensing as a possible Special Products business category, Kapp was looking far outside the traditional Special Products box; when WSP landed and consolidated all of Warner's synch business in 1983, WSP jumped over Columbia Special Products, who would never even make a bid to handle CBS's synch business, before Sony (who acquired CBS) launched its own synch department a couple of years later.

Beginning in the late 1970s, Kapp noticed that more licensed masters were appearing in films and TV shows. At first it was a mere trickle but, in the aftermath of *Saturday Night Fever*, it seemed to be gaining momentum.

The record labels had never demonstrated any concern for this area, and, given the priorities labels' Business Affairs people worked under, the labels were not equipped to handle even this small uptick in synch licensing activity. "When a synch request came into the Business Affairs department," recalls Fukuyama, "it was always put at the bottom of the pile. A synch request was a nuisance that a Business Affairs person would try to ignore as long as possible." Kapp saw a trend developing, in terms of the increased interest in licensing masters for film and TV, and he wanted to get ahead of the train; so he approached the labels and offered not only to take synch off their hands, but also to make a real business out of it. The heads of Warner Bros., Elektra, and Atlantic as well as Warner corporate signed off, and the WSP synch department was launched in 1983. Fukuyama says,

> When I started at WSP, no other record label had a dedicated synch person, and there were still labels who handled synch inquiries by forwarding calls to a recorded message which gave instructions on how to send requests in *by mail*.
>
> We couldn't have launched at a better time. We were up and running with all of the major film and TV clients, and with our labels and artists, so we were ready when the first turning point came, and that was the debut of *Miami Vice* in 1984. Harry Garfield, who handled music clearance for Universal Television, had told me excitedly (and often) that this was the show that was going to single-handedly revolutionize the use of licensed masters on television. I told Harry to let everyone on the production know that they could count us in. We pounced. Harry was right. *Vice* changed the use of music in television immediately, and forever. The music was a big part of every show. The series was a hit right off the bat and the music played an instrumental role in its success. We did everything possible to get Michael Mann whatever he wanted. Which wasn't always easy, because it was a high-volume show asking for a wide array of top-shelf masters under tight deadlines. But it was all worth it. *Vice* opened the floodgates for TV shows to use licensed masters.

When WSP took over synch, fees were low, from years of low demand and, frankly, Business Affairs people agreeing to low fees just to get these deals off their desks. No real effort had been made to negotiate good fees or to get the fees up, and no label had ever developed a synch business strategy of any kind. However, we had promised the labels that we would treat synch as if it was our primary business and to grow the business by raising fees and aggressively pursuing opportunities. Fortunately, the demand for masters increased, and that enabled us to raise fees rapidly without much resistance from the studios and TV producers. (Our original five-year plan was to increase fees by 25% year-over-year for the first five years, and then reassess. We met that goal easily.) This was the era of MTV's emergence as a cultural phenomenon and the unprecedented popularity of artists like Michael Jackson, Madonna, Prince, Phil Collins, etc., so musical awareness and the glamor attributed to popular music were at an all-time high. The studios recognized all this, of course, and wanted a piece of it, even if only to license more masters for their films and TV shows. While the wind was definitely at our backs, in terms of the time being right to raise fees, I believe that there was one factor that probably greatly accelerated the process: the mid-1980s explosion in soundtrack albums for blockbuster films, which motivated film studios to spend money on licensed masters as well as masters created specifically for the film; in addition to the obvious goal of releasing an album that might sell millions of units, the studios could justify much bigger music budgets on the premise that, even if the album didn't turn a big profit, the music was still helping to cross-promote the film, and helping the film reach a wider audience. (This being the Reagan years, the studios seemed to apply 'trickle down' economics by increasing music budgets for even their less-than-blockbuster projects.) This was the golden age of MTV videos that intercut an artist's performance with movie clips. Although the big-money soundtrack album era was over by the early 1990s, that era's dramatic increase in music budgets—and therefore license fees for music—would have a lasting impact for years to come.

With the number of license requests and pitch opportunities having multiplied exponentially since the launch of WSP's synch department in 1983, WSP started to add personnel. In 1988, Fukuyama hired Tom Rowland, who, within five years, would be running the synch department at MCA Special Markets (MCA would eventually become Universal); almost 25 years later, with Universal now the largest record company in the world, Tom still heads the department.

During the 1980s and 1990s the soundtrack business became a big business. Films wanted to have enough music to fill an album because the studios saw the commercially released soundtracks as another way to promote their films. The productions would be given much larger budgets if they could build in a marketable soundtrack. MTV was also growing into a powerful force for selling music and the labels were spending hundreds of thousands of dollars on a single music video. (Music videos are considered a marketing expense; labels charge back a portion of the cost to the artist for the making of the video.) The music video was a great tool for promoting a song used in a film, so the film companies really wanted to align themselves with record labels and publishers. Film companies would make music videos to promote their film and include clips from the film. This led to more commercial music being licensed for use in films. It was a symbiotic relationship—film companies would want to produce a soundtrack, which provided money to the labels, and the record labels would find exposure for their artists in films.

One such film that became a ginormous success was Don Simpson and Jerry Bruckheimer's 1986 blockbuster *Top Gun*. This hit was important to the music business because all of a sudden there was serious money being allocated to secure the right songs into a film. Select songs from the *Top Gun* soundtrack include:

- "Danger Zone" by Kenny Loggins;
- "Mighty Wings" by Cheap Trick;
- "Playing with the Boys" by Kenny Loggins;
- "Heaven in Your Eyes" by Loverboy;
- "Through the Fire" by Larry Greene;

- "Destination Unknown" by Marietta;
- "Hot Summer Nights" by Miami Sound Machine;
- "Lead Me On" by Teena Marie;
- "Take My Breath Away (Love Theme from *Top Gun*)" by Berlin.

(There was also a 1999 special edition release and then a 2006 deluxe edition release, each with bonus tracks.)

Although many songs were written for the screen and then sold via a soundtrack recording, labels began realizing that a film could help expose a previously recorded song, which in turn would bring attention to the artist and could be spun as PR for raising artist awareness. Recording artists signed to exclusive record deals were then able to exploit their songs in films.

As the film and television industries evolved, more and more use of pre-recorded music became available for creative directors to incorporate. This was terrific for the artist, since it showed they were keen to collaborate with other creative types. Likewise, and more importantly, the labels were generating more ancillary income through the licensing of music for use in motion pictures.

As the film industry became more developed, there became an increased need for pre-recorded music in film productions. Hiring a composer is, and always has been, the most cost-effective way to secure music for any film production, and many famous films have wonderful scores, such as *The Mission*, *The Social Network*, *Drive*, *Shaft* and thousands more. Yet there are also many successful movies that are comprised of memorable music soundtracks, such as *Little Miss Sunshine*, *Garden State*, *Twilight* and many, many more. There are even labels that specialize in soundtrack releases, such as Milan Records, Varèse Sarabande and Hollywood Records.

Then recording artists were beginning to be asked to write songs specifically for films. One such example is the James Bond series. Each film brings in a top recording artist to write a unique song for the film which then gets released on a commercially available soundtrack.

Some classic examples of original songs composed specifically for film or television include:

- "Raindrops Keep Fallin' on My Head," performed by B.J. Thomas in *Butch Cassidy and the Sundance Kid*;
- "Theme from *Shaft*," performed by Isaac Hayes in *Shaft*;
- "Nobody Does It Better," performed by Carly Simon in *The Spy Who Loved Me*;
- "Moon River," performed by Audrey Hepburn in *Breakfast at Tiffany's*;
- "A View to a Kill," performed by Duran Duran in *A View to a Kill*;
- "Live and Let Die," performed by Paul McCartney and Wings in *Live and Let Die*.

Many original songs are written and recorded with a specific film in mind. The B.J. Thomas version of "Raindrops Keep Fallin' on My Head" heard in *Butch Cassidy and the Sundance Kid* was written by Burt Bacharach and Hal David in 1969. The score was recorded when B.J. had a cold, and the producers were reluctant to include it. However, the placement of the song and the success of the film drew attention and it became a hit on the Billboard charts.

Other songs that became hits after the release of a film include:

- "Skyfall"—Adele, from *Skyfall*;
- "Tubular Bells"—Mike Oldfield, from *The Exorcist*;
- "Lose Yourself"—Eminem, from *8 Mile*;
- "When Doves Cry"—Prince, from *Purple Rain*;
- "Stayin' Alive"—The Bee Gees, from *Saturday Night Fever*;
- "Jai Ho (You Are My Destiny)"—A.R. Rahman and The Pussycat Dolls featuring Nicole Scherzinger, from *Slumdog Millionaire*.

Since both soundtracks and compilations are different from an artist's primary discography, labels began to employ individuals to handle these types of requests. Those recruits were either affiliated with the Business Affairs or Legal departments. Over time, the labels created a new department called Special Markets. It is this department, which still exists today, that has proliferated from less than a handful of employees to employing dozens of persons to handle the mounting synchronization requests for music used in media. These are all ancillary income-generating requests. Universal Music,

Warner Music Group and Sony Music seemingly have dozens of employees manning the creative and synch desks. This little area has ballooned into significant income for both labels and publishers, and with the consolidation of labels there are mounting catalogs of content that are becoming more difficult for the behemoths to oversee.

Some smaller labels still operate independently and usually do most of the release functions for new albums. But below is a select list of the various label imprints controlled by the three United States conglomerates:

Sony Music Entertainment	Warner Music Group	Universal Music Group	
Arista	Asylum	A&M	Angel
Columbia	Atlantic	Decca	Astralwerks
Epic	Elektra	Def Jam	Blue Note
Legacy	Maverick	Deutsche Grammophon	Capitol
RCA	Nonesuch	Geffen	Liberty
Roc Nation	Reprise	Interscope	Manhattan
Ultra	Rhino	Island	Parlophone
Verity	Roadrunner	Lost Highway	Relentless
	Sire	Mercury	Republic
		Motown	Vertigo
		Polydor	Verve
		Republic	Virgin

Today, when locating and clearing music for a media production or compilation it is very important to locate the original release of a recording. This will be the original owner, not the company that released a compilation. For example, the Sony soundtrack to *Garden State* includes the Nick Drake song "One of These Things First." This song can also be found on the 2007 Time Life compilation release "Four Decades of Folk Rock." Now, if you were to use this song in your film where would you go? Time Life? Or Sony? Neither. You would have to do the research and discover that first of all Nick Drake died at age 24 and only released three records, all on the Hannibal label, from 1969–1972. Hannibal Records was then purchased in the 1990s by the amazingly creative Midwest label Rykodisc, which was later sold to Island Records' supreme leader Chris Blackwell. His label Palm Pictures (known for releasing soundtrack albums) purchased Rykodisc, which was then bought by Warner Music. This is a roundabout way of saying that you would ultimately discover that to license Nick Drake's song "One of These Things First" you would now have to reach out to WSP, not Sony or Time Life.

Then, to request the song in a compilation there are certain requirements a master holder needs to know before it can grant you a quote. Generally, compilation albums quote on a per-unit basis, so a request will look like the following:

We would like to secure a master use license for the following:

Licensor Name and Address:	Joe Schmo, 123 Little Rock Road, Kansas, MI
Compilation Title:	Dad's Favorite Songs
Track Requested:	I Left My Heart in San Francisco
Rights Required:	Non-exclusive
Territory:	Worldwide
Term:	10 years
Number of Titles:	28 tracks total—2 discs
Format:	LP, DD (as full album) via website only
Distribution:	Retail, mail order, digital
Royalty Rate:	$0.05
Club Rate:	N/A
Full Dealer Price:	$40.00
Advance:	4,000 units or $200.00 per master with rollovers
Accounting:	Bi-annual
Release Date:	4th Quarter 2017
Other Relevant Information:	A crowdfunding campaign is being implemented to raise funds for the release
Estimated Sales:	4,000 units

This sort of request can be used for requesting music from major and independent labels. Both constituents price about the same for compilation albums. In the synchronization use territory, independent labels are generally easier to work with because, although they function in much the same way, they have a smaller infrastructure, closer relationships with their artists and not so many corporate layers. For example, Warner was purchased by Access Industries, led by Soviet-born Leonard Blavatnik. It is now part of a conglomerate that owns or has invested in Deezer, Tory Burch, Songkick and EP Energy, among other oil, gas and real estate companies. Independent label Epitaph, for example, was started by guitarist Brett Gurewitz from the band Bad Religion to release their own records, but has since grown into a reputable indie label for punk and emo bands and has stayed truly independent. Speaking to someone at the label and getting permission to use music in either a film, TV or ad production or in a compilation takes a fifth of the time it does when dealing with any major label. The folks at Epitaph are friendly, return phone calls and, best of all, respond quickly. Other independent labels with great reputations are: ATO, Beggars Group, Concord Music Group, Daptone Records, Domino, eOne, Ghostly International, Luaka Bop, Mack Avenue Records, Naxos, Six Degrees, Sub Pop, Third Side, Tommy Boy, Yep Roc and many more.

The main difference between the independent label and the major is the access and ability to negotiate a deal swifter and at, generally, a more agreeable fee. Fewer corporate layers and internal approvals are needed. Yet the goal of both the independent and major label is to exploit their catalogs, and therefore any third-party licensing is very important to them, especially during this time when retail sales of recorded music appear to be decreasing.

4

MUSIC SUPERVISORS

Every Project Can Use a Little Music Supervision

By now you may be a bit confused and realize that music rights can be daunting. Well, if that seems to be the case you can always enlist someone called a **music supervisor**. These lovely people can do a range of duties to alleviate the labyrinth of music clearance, and help media producers zero-in on what they need creatively. These individuals generally work with a team of colleagues, especially those who work on television shows or large-budget films, and can access all genres and styles of music instantaneously. They are sleuths, detectives, negotiators and puzzle-lovers. They are music nerds who you'd most likely find seeking out the local record shop while touring a new city rather than seeing the major attractions. They relish looking at record spines to find catalog numbers and authentic release dates. When listening to music they can detect the artist, style, era and genre without looking at their iPod, phone or Sonos system. If they do look, it's only to confirm what they thought they knew!

Music supervisors are a mysterious breed. Most have come to the job via happenstance or luck. Another handful started down this path after working at a record label or publisher. Another faction come from radio. Yet whatever their path, they are very passionate and knowledgeable about music.

They play in bands, collect records, obsess over remastered reissues, listen incessantly to music and are esteemed by the people around them as the go-to music source.

What a lot of people don't know is that much of what a music supervisor does pertains to budget and negotiating deals with copyright holders. It's not all about the music. Supervisors make their living handling the business side of music and knowing who to contact in order to get what they need. About 75% of the job consists of dealing with music licensing, procurement, staying on budget, delivering the correct metadata and handling a range of personalities with different needs. For a fraction of music supervisors, the work is creative, and even then that can be hampered by rights issues.

So, what is a music supervisor and what do they really do? They are music experts who assist media producers with sourcing the right music for their project within budget. They broker deals between the production and the music rights owners. These individuals, generally independent contractors (unless they work in-house or on staff at a production company), are not affiliated with a label or publisher. They have a non-partisan relationship to catalogs. Their goal is to source the appropriate music and deliver it according to the legal requirements of the production team. Their job description on a film is considered **below-the-line**, which is any crew member involved in a film except the actors, director, producers, and writers, and these folks should be recommended or sized up to see if they fit the project.

Figure 4.1 Guild of Music Supervisors

The Guild of Music Supervisors—a non-profit organization with the mission to promote the craft of music supervision for the mutual benefit of all media stakeholders in film, television, games, advertising, trailers and emerging media—defines the role of a music supervisor as "a qualified professional who oversees all music-related aspects of film, television, advertising, video games and other existing or emerging visual media platforms as required" (see www.guildofmusicsupervisors.com/the-role). In addition, the Guild says,

1. The music supervisor must possess a comprehensive knowledge of how music impacts the visual medium. The music supervisor works with the key decision makers and/or designated creative team to collectively determine the musical vision, tone and style that best suits the project.
2. The music supervisor provides professional-quality service that combines creative, technical and management expertise with relevant proven experience. This specialized combination of diversified knowledge and unique skills is integrated into all stages of development, pre-production, production, post-production, delivery and strategic marketing of the project with regard to all music-related elements.

The Guild further defines the supervisor's responsibilities as:

1. Identify, secure and supervise any and all music related talent, which includes composers, songwriters, recording artists, on-camera performers, musicians, orchestrators, arrangers, copyists, contractors, music producers, engineers, etc.: liaise and negotiate with talent representation, including legal, label, talent management, agency, business management, etc.
2. Liaise and effectively communicate with other related and involved professionals and support staff, i.e., directorial, production, editorial, sound (production and post), camera, choreography, studio and network executives, advertising agencies, clients, label

executives, game designers, distributors and cross-promotional marketing partners.
3. Possess an accurate knowledge of all costs associated with delivery of music elements. Determine and advise on financial needs of projects and generate realistic budget with respect to all music related costs. Deliver all required music elements within the established budgetary parameters.
4. Advise on feasibility of schedule based on release, broadcast, campaign or product delivery. Deliver all music elements consistent with specific technical requirements. Manage and/or secure legal rights of new and existing recordings, clearance of synchronization and master use licenses of pre-existing music, credits, cue sheets, etc. within scheduling parameters.
5. Determine the viability of, creation of and securing exposure or distribution of any music related ancillary product, i.e., soundtrack, single, video, Internet downloads, etc. for the purpose of promotion or additional revenue streams.

Not all music supervisors will know everything about all genres of music, but they should have the resources at hand to source what is needed for a project. They should know where to go when asked, for example, to find Appalachian music. We are called to work on numerous projects that are country-specific, like *Meet the Patels* (India) or *Nasser's Republic* (Egypt). Although we're not ethnomusicologists nor profess to be, the key is to have trusted resources and the ability to reach out to those who specialize in music from those countries. We cull their opinions, confirm the research and then present it to a client. Media producers sometimes don't have the time or resources to find the appropriate track or song for a scene. Thus, the music supervisor's job is to be a reliable source to satisfy that request and keep the producer on budget. Music elevates the mood of a scene or makes reference to a certain time and place, and can help transition from one sequence to another. So it is important to get the audio flavor just right.

A qualified music supervisor should also truly understand the clearance process, whether they provide that service or not. **Clearance**—the process of securing consent from the appropriate rights holders—and the ability to secure a piece of selected music within a client's budget are essential. There is nothing worse than suggesting a piece of music to a client and then discovering the license fee is approved at three times higher than expected. Granted, there will be times when a filmmaker, or client, desires a piece of music that cannot be cleared. For a Netflix documentary series, the Patsy Cline recording "You Belong to Me" could not be cleared for the same fee as the Pops Staples song "Better Home," so the song had to be removed. It may then become the job of the music supervisor to make alternative suggestions or glean information on why the song was not authorized, so the client can make informed decisions during the process.

Occasionally denials can be turned around to become an approval. This is called a 'reversal' and it takes a good music supervisor to see an opportunity in to order to achieve one. Knowing the sensibilities of the parties you are negotiating with is important. We had one instance when a client received a denial for the use of LCD Soundsystem's "Dance Yrself Clean" in an epic urban ski scene in the action sports documentary *All.I.Can*.

The request went out and it was denied by management. There were also some rights issues among the band, who were no longer together. The filmmakers built the scene around this music. In the now-infamous 'street segment' where the late J.P. Auclair skis Canadian urban back alleys, the filmmakers pleaded with the artists directly by making a video. "We needed to get the clip in front of the band, and let them see and hear the piece," recounts director David Mossap of Sherpa Cinema. "We sent a video plea to management along with the clip, and the music was soon approved." So in this case, the band changed their mind and the denial was then switched to an approval.

Unfortunately, our office also saw an appeal turn sour. We want to stress that this does not happen often, yet when it does it leaves an indelible demerit on the artist for future potential licensing opportunities. Our particular situation arose when an action sports client requested the use of the Nine Inch Nails song "The Day the World Went Away" (written by Trent Reznor) for use in its trailer of an upcoming ski film. Management

Figure 4.2 *All.I.Can*—Sherpas Cinema, 2011

requested to see the visual and so it was sent. The song was approved contingent on their review of the final edit. (That sort of condition happens, but it's unusual.) The client locked the song and sent it back, yet the names of its sponsors now appeared at the end—as is typical for an action sports film—and upon seeing this management denied the use. The publisher responded by saying, "I just got word from Trent's lawyer and at this stage they're going to respectfully pass. Super sorry for the inconvenience. I was really trying to get this done for you." This is an uncommon situation, but it reinforces the scrutiny management can place on a particular placement. The song had to be removed and due to time constraints the composer had to create something new for the trailer.

A good music supervisor must be a good negotiator. They know when to push forward and when to pull back when dealing with major labels, publishers and occasionally managers. They know who the stubborn and prickly ones are, the curmudgeons, and those who love getting deals done quickly. They also know which artists will and will not respond. They are familiar with the companies and artists hungry for placement and those who couldn't care less. Many times a supervisor will have one bite at the apple, and so transparency and accuracy are important.

Music supervisor Gary Calamar (*Six Feet Under*, *True Blood*, and *Dexter*) recounts the difficulties and peculiarities of using Led Zeppelin's music.

> We used two Led Zeppelin songs in *True Blood*. The band has an unusual policy that if your request is accepted by the label and publisher, and management approves the use, then you must use the song. Now these songs are very expensive...something like $100K/side. Many times a supervisor will clear two or three songs so the producer has a choice. In Led Zeppelin's case if they sign off and approve, you have to use the piece and you have to pay them within seven days. In *True Blood* we used two different songs on two different episodes.

Do the math!

Whether negotiating the rights for classic mega-hits or indie, unsigned bands, music supervisors have to tread lightly and play their cards just right in order to get the outcome they desire.

For the 2005 film *Roll Bounce*, New York-based music supervisor Barry Cole shared a story about clearing Donna Summer's stirring hit disco song

Figure 4.3 Music Supervisor Gary Calamar

"Love to Love You Baby." Since the movie was a period film set in the 1970s, Cole wanted to use this song in a particular scene.

> Summer had turned religious and did not want the song used. So we put together a package with as much ammunition as possible, because the movie was really a coming-of-age roller-skating movie

and it took place in the 1970s. We were looking for music of the period and the film was about 14 to 15 year olds roller-skating. After we sent the package we then received an approval to license the song because Donna Summer's children liked the main character.

It was just one of those things where you have a song which is not the easiest to clear but you put as much forward as possible and be as open as possible.

On the Peter Bratt documentary *Dolores*, we had a situation arise while clearing the very difficult James Brown song "Say It Loud—I'm Black and I'm Proud." The publisher wanted more money than the budget could afford, and therefore we had to talk to Brown's estate representative. The documentary was about the United Farm Workers union's Dolores Huerta, and we discovered that the estate rep had actually picketed grapes at a Safeway in San Francisco back in the 1960s under Dolores' command. Once he knew what the film was about, and saw the scene involved, it was a no-brainer, and the fee came down to the budgeted **MFN** (**most favored nations**—see Chapter 6 for more details). These sorts of reversals and approvals happen due to the music supervisor's diligence, relationships and transparency. The cost of hiring one can save a producer more money than trying to do the clearance in-house, on their own.

If requested, too, a music supervisor can compile a **soundtrack album** for a film. This is generally a CD or digital download release of the songs heard within a film, or 'inspired by' the film. The supervisor's relationships with numerous record labels means they can reach out to their colleagues within the industry to secure a soundtrack deal. These deals are handled differently than securing synchronization licenses. How a soundtrack benefits a filmmaker depends on the nature of a project. For low-budget films, soundtracks can bring in additional income to help with post-production costs because the label that releases the compilation recording can provide an 'advance,' or sum of money, to the production company when it delivers the masters for use on a soundtrack. Other times, a label may desire to release a soundtrack album in conjunction with a film since it may already have a handful of songs licensed in the film, and it is an easy way to

56 MUSIC SUPERVISORS

Figure 4.4 The Life Aquatic soundtrack cover

promote their artists. There are all sorts of soundtrack albums and although these compilations generally don't garner huge sales, there have been some stellar stand-outs like The Hunger Games; Garden State; O Brother, Where Art Thou?; Saturday Night Fever; Crazy Heart; The Life Aquatic with Steve Zissou and many, many more.

The supervisor's job is all about relationships.

James Keach has directed and produced documentaries such as Glen Campbell: I'll Be Me and the feature film Walk the Line. He had this piece of advice:

> Work with music supervisors who have good relationships in licensing for movies because the guys that do the licensing on the day-to-day basis usually have pretty good relationships with people, and they'll

Figure 4.5 Producer, Director James Keach

give a young filmmaker good advice and say that you can't afford that, or if you do, this is the way you have to do it. Be sure to consult with people who have been down this road before because it can very quickly turn into no before you've even had a chance to talk about it.

Do not turn to your friend who has amazing musical taste. He may be able to soundtrack your film, but he may not know the first thing about who to contact or how to close a deal.

A supervisor who is consistently working is constantly in communication with music agents, publishers, labels and managers. Their days are filled with emails from licensors. They get to know these people well. They also know who has moved on from one shop to the next, and who the new contacts are. A good supervisor is also someone who will give you sound advice and steer you away from roadblocks. "I've heard many stories about Bob Dylan not wanting to license his music," Keach recounts. Our office recently found it difficult to negotiate and clear several Neil Diamond songs for a documentary. This made it terribly difficult for the filmmaker to move forward with his film, so it's important that your supervisor be able to tell you this. You don't want to be deep into production of a Dylan documentary only to uncover that he will never license his music to you. Especially with music documentaries and bio pics, Keach explains, "The artist or estate needs to be on board early because they can use the music as leverage."

Music supervisors are sleuths and will go to great lengths to get a song cleared. Randall Poster, who has supervised television shows like *Boardwalk Empire* and *Vinyl*, as well as the films *The Great Gatsby*, *The Grand Budapest Hotel*, *The Hangover* and *The Wolf of Wall Street*, recalls,

> There was a situation where we wanted to include an Italian pop song. We had a copy of a 45rpm record, but the label we couldn't find. It was classic—prompting the Italians to really hustle for us. The archive is in Naples, in the basement of this building, and there was a flood. The performer had died and so we tried to find his daughter. Ultimately we were connected to the family somehow through the daughter's husband's hairdresser, and we finally found our way to license the piece.

Supervisors can also revive old recordings, dust them off and bring them to light for new audiences to hear. Poster recalls his experience working on the HBO series *Boardwalk Empire*, where Season 1 was set in the 1920s.

A lot of those recordings had been dormant for 80 to 90 years. We would find ourselves in situations where we would have to convince the record companies that they actually owned it. They had no sense of what they had, especially with all the various consolidations of companies.

A similar situation with our office when we attempted to clear two Radha Krishna Temple tracks for a documentary about the Hare Krishna movement. Approval needed to be granted from Apple Records, now controlled by Universal. However, it could not locate the tracks in its system. So one of the member-musicians of the Radha Krishna Temple group who performed on the specific recording wrote the following appeal:

I am one of the members of the Radha Krishna Temple rock band and was one of the musicians that took part in the recording of the songs "Hare Krishna Mantra" and "Govindam" in 1967 with George Harrison as the composer, fellow musician and friend.
We are trying to license these songs to the film "Hare Krishna," a documentary on the life of our Spiritual Master, Bhaktivedanta Swami Prabhupada. These are ancient mantra songs, and are freely given to everyone. We would very much appreciate a gratis use of these two songs being granted to the filmmakers, as it would be helpful to their budget.
I also hear you are having difficulty locating the copyright holders. Since I am a member of the group and we did this recording, it is important for our constituency to secure these rights properly. If you need a quitclaim deed, I would be happy to provide it.

To get the deal done, the member was suggesting that the label issue a **quitclaim** deed, a legal document where an interest in a copyright is being transferred. However, unlike a legal license, a quitclaim deed carries no promise of ownership. It's basically saying, 'I make no representations or warranty covering your use of the music, and that if I in fact do own it, then I am giving you permission to use it. But if I do not own it, you're on your own.' It should be noted that this situation is really unusual. People are not quick to issue quitclaim deeds and producers are not jumping on opportunities to secure them in lieu of a license. But a good supervisor would know that this option exists out there, and if all else fails, one could try and secure a quitclaim deed to get a deal done. The supervisor should consult legal counsel to see what it (the production) feels comfortable doing before exploring this option.

All in all, a music supervisor can be an asset to any production—big or small. They have the relationships and know who to contact. They 'speak the speak' and get deals done. They can help find replacement music with boatloads of creative solutions at hand. Most importantly, they keep the music budget in check and help deliver all the music legally. They are a strategic partner worth the investment.

5

FINDING MUSIC

A Community of Composers, Libraries and Representatives

Finding the right music for any production is always a challenge. Where do you start? There are numerous platforms and websites, and a gazillion creative directions to go in. There are songs that would be terrific to incorporate into a production but are way out of a budget. There might be other songs on the web that have no contact information, making the task of locating the copyright holder impossible. There may be changes in the script, or changes in the production personnel, or changes in the vision and intent of the piece which, of course, may change the music selection.

"Our choice of music is based on the creative and the monetary," says music supervisor Todd Porter of the advertising agency Goodby Silverstein,

> I had an experience where I spent three weeks getting various artists to cover a Carpenters song and found out that ultimately no one could do it better than the Carpenters.
>
> With a song whose lyrics are meaningful, I'll get initial quotes for the publishing and then we begin the process of finding other artists to cover the song to get a natural-sounding piece. Or we lip-synch to the song with actors, or if we need a specific sound we engage a music house.

These are just a few of the ways music is procured for use in an ad campaign, and it is the same for use in films.

There are three main resources to obtain music for any production: (1) hire a composer to create original music; (2) source music from a **production music library**; or (3) license commercial music or popular, pre-recorded music.

HIRE A COMPOSER

One of the most efficient and affordable ways to get music for your production is to hire a composer. There are numerous composers in almost any city worldwide ready and willing to work on a film or commercial production. The key is to find an individual who can work within a designated budget and whose music aligns with the director's vision. Get references, make notes about a composer's past work and definitely listen to demo reels. There is nothing worse than 'getting in bed' with a composer who soon after you must 'chase out of the room.'

Figure 5.1 Miriam Cutler in her studio

Source: Photo by Mark Hanauer

In the motion picture, television, commercial and documentary industry composers are considered as below-the-line. This refers to anyone who is not an actor, director, writer or producer. They generally work for hire and receive a flat fee. Composers must deliver a set duration of music (30 minutes, 40 minutes, etc.) on a designated 'delivery' day in a determined format (DAT, MP4s, AIFF, WAV files, etc.). The negotiated fee will include the cost of all the budgeted musicians, studio time and any ancillary costs related to delivering the music.

Many composers feel directors come to them too late in the game. So when should a composer be brought into a project? Timing will depend on the state of the film. Some producers get far down the road and then realize they must hire a composer and do so during post-production and editing. Other times, the composer is considered when the script is finalized and the director has thoughts about the mood and tone of the film.

Seasoned composer Miriam Cutler, who has worked on over a hundred independent and documentary films including *The Hunting Game* and *Ghosts of Abu Ghraib*, says,

> I always tell filmmakers when an audience goes into a theater, they go to see something and hear something. It doesn't matter how many years you've been working on it, how much research you did, or who the actors are. If the music is not up to the highest standard or has not been well thought out, it will ultimately dilute the vision of your film.

Generally, a composer and sound designer should be contracted around the same time an editor is considered.

Berlin-based Golden Globe award-winning composer Jóhann Jóhannsson, who scored Hollywood films *Arrival*, *Prisoners*, *Sicario* and *The Theory of Everything*, says his long-standing relationship with director Denis Villeneuve, with whom he worked on *Arrival* and *Prisoners*, likes to work with Jóhannsson early on in the process.

Villeneuve discovered Jóhannsson from his live performances.

"Film composing is something I've done on the side," says Jóhannsson of his solo recording career, "I've tried to balance the two." Over the last three

Figure 5.2 Jóhann Jóhannsson
Source: Photo by Jónatan Grétarsson

to four years, more of Jóhannsson's work has leaned toward film. "I haven't always been able to keep to that balance, but that is changing again now."

The score of Prisoners rings most closely to Jóhannsson's work as a recording artist. "Denis Villeneuve chose to work with me because he heard my performance work and album work. That is the sound he wanted."

"On Denis' film Arrival, I'm part of the project before he starts shooting. I read the script and he shares the art work and design with me. With Sicario and Prisoners, I was able to visit the set," Jóhannsson reminisces,

> For *Sicario* it was important to get a sense of the locations and the geography of the film, atmosphere and physical sense of place… where the film is set.
>
> With Denis I also try to write things early on. For example, for *Prisoners* and for *Arrival* I wrote a number of pieces before we started shooting, so he was listening to my music when he was shooting, and a couple of those pieces become an important part of the score.

Figure 5.3 Arrival—2016

For *Arrival* Jóhannsson not only scored original work, but two cues incorporate the essence and feel of avant-garde "legend" (as Jóhannsson describes her) Joan La Barbara's 1980 piece "Erin."

For the one point in the film where there is a montage of predictions about the future, Jóhannsson pays homage to La Barbara by recreating her repetitive vocal incantations, which provide an amazing lengthy aural

Figure 5.4 Joan La Barbara
Source: © 2009 Mark Mahaney

backdrop to the scene. The piece returns over the closing credits, taking the viewer into an incredible paralleled sound and visual experience. Jóhannsson says, "The film is about language and communication and how language affects the way we think and experience time. Therefore my score is very much centered around vocals." Jóhannsson's ode to La Barbara's work is spectacular.

For Miriam Cutler, who works on more-limited-budget film projects, time constraints become a factor. "Many times directors think about music too late in the game," she reflects,

> [c]omposers, editors and sound designers should start communicating at the beginning and come up with a work flow or communication process so that everybody is on the same page. I think what happens a lot of times is that music and sound are left to the very end, and by then, the filmmakers are in a crunch to finish.

"Sometimes you may be joining a project that the filmmaker, producer and director have been working on for years," says Jóhannsson. "When you join them during the last months of a project you basically absorb a lot of things quickly, and figure out what they are trying to say."

Generally, when a composer is contracted to write for a production, their deals are considered '**work-for-hire**' and the rights to the music are held by the employer. This sort of deal is more commonly found with large studio productions and some television networks.

More often, original music will be composed for a production and then licensed into the production so the rights remain with the composer. This type of deal is more commonly found with low-budget and independent films.

"My model is for me to own my music," Cutler states adamantly, "I've scored well over 100 films, in which I own all my music except on six films." Only those six projects are owned by HBO. "With all the other films, I am then able to collect the back-end." This ability to 'collect on the back-end' pertains to the public performance monies that a composer collects from their **performing rights organizations** (BMI, ASCAP or SESAC in the United States) due to the repeat performance of the film. Performance rights organizations collect royalties for the re-airing of a film on television and outside of the United States in theaters, and, in recent years, performance royalties have been collected for the re-airing of a production over the Internet. With television viewership declining and more users watching films and series on the Internet, we are now entering an age where significant income from back-end performance may be negligible.

Although Cutler has earned substantial royalty income from the re-airing of her older films on television, she senses this sort of 'mail money' may not be available to younger composers who are now being contracted to create music for shows on Netflix, Hulu, Mubi, Amazon Prime, Refinery29 and other Internet-only companies. She asserts,

> There is no way that the economic model on streaming sites is going to be sustainable right now. Once the digital world takes over, it will drive the price down. There is a ton of work out there, and getting four-cent royalty checks is not sustainable.

Cutler shared an example of the difference of her pay from performance royalties for the re-airing of a show in 2016. She earned $3,107.87 from a CNN broadcast of the show, compared to $61.66 for an Amazon exhibition of the show.

Emmy Award-winning composer Jeff Beal (*House of Cards, Monk*) says,

> In the low-budget world, when you are talking about non-fiction or independent films, one thing a filmmaker can do to sweeten the pie is to offer the composer the publishing side of the music. I ask for that quite frequently and get it granted to me on the more independent films.

"We are also in a new frontier where digital is becoming the most popular model of distribution," continues Beal, "so all content creators are having an active discussion and debate on how to best monetize their intellectual property across all these platforms, whether they are broadcast or online." Some online streaming companies are approaching composers and giving them money to buy-out their rights. This does not allow for the composer to make back-end money from their performing rights organization, and can be a concern for newer composers.

If dwindling royalties due to Internet streaming persist, it will be very important for composers to start asking for a larger up-front commission fee. In general, composers and media producers will be better off if they address issues of budget and delivery at the outset of their negotiation. If an orchestral score is desired, then a bigger budget and time must be figured into the equation. When Miriam Cutler speaks to filmmakers she says that it really comes down to what the filmmaker wants to accomplish. "Be realistic and do your homework," she emphasizes. "Talk to other composers and filmmakers whose music you liked. Make an informed decision; don't be wishful. When you go below a certain amount of money, it is impossible to accomplish what is needed."

Generally, when a composer is hired for a studio project, the fee is an 'all-in' or 'buy-out' of the rights. This ensures that the employer can use the music in their production to be exhibited in all media. If an employer has a limited budget, the publishing rights are often retained by the composer. This way the composer can potentially make more money via public broadcast or reuse in the future. This does not affect the fee to the employer, but allows for additional monies for the composer, should the project become successful.

Another common scenario is when the composer accepts the fee but translates that fee into a license. This means that the employer will be able to use the music in the context of the work that they are being commissioned for. Full ownership of the master and publishing stays with the composer. This is beneficial to both parties because the media producer can use the music in their production for all media and the composer has the ability to re-license the music to other producers after a period of time, generally about two years. It helps the composer generate more money from their back catalog and helps keep the cost down for the person hiring.

"It's important for me to come up with something that we both like to work with, so I start with having a discussion about what their ideas are," recounts Cutler who, like many composers, sends a deal memo document.

> I tell my clients about the process, where the money is going to be spent, all my technical specs and other details. It's an incredibly helpful tool. Then [we] have a discussion based on any questions they have. It's important to engage them, and it is a process like editing. Finding the right music is deep, so [we] have to be on the same page and telling the same story.

"I lived in Denmark for eight years and scored a lot of documentaries," recounts Jóhann Jóhannsson. "[For] projects on a smaller size, I generally license the score and keep the publishing and master rights. But it is impossible when you are dealing with the Hollywood films I work on now."

The main points of a composer agreement pertain to: (1) the amount of music to be delivered; (2) the date of first submission, rewrite, and delivery; (3) the amount of rewrites; (4) the publishing and recording ownership; and (5) the fee and payment structure. A contract will then follow with these points:

1. Services rendered
2. Fee
3. Payment schedule
4. Credit
5. Ownership of master and copyright
6. Synchronization and master use license (if deemed necessary)
7. Out-of-context promo use
8. Soundtrack album
9. Expenses.

Here is a sample composer agreement:

MUSIC COMPOSITION AGREEMENT

This Agreement is made and entered into this ___ day of _____, 20__, by and between _____ ('Producer'), and _____ ('Composer'), respecting the composition, production, use and ownership of music for use in and in connection with the film '_____' by Producer.
The parties hereby agree as follows:

1. The Producer has commissioned Composer to compose original music and Composer shall produce, record and deliver a master recording of the Music (the 'Master') suitable for synchronization by Producer.
2. In exchange for the services to be performed by Composer, as well as all expenses incurred by Composer in connection therewith, and the rights conveyed in this Agreement, producer shall pay Composer $_____.

This amount will be paid in thirds, in which $____.00 will be paid upon signing; $_____.00 will be paid upon acceptance and delivery; and the third $____.00 will be paid upon completion of the mix of the Master. It is understood that if the production exceeds twelve (12) months due to reasons in control of Producer an additional fee will be discussed. While Composer maintains all rights of creative control, Composer will, in good faith, take into account Producer's opinions and beliefs regarding the Music.

3. Composer hereby covenants, warrants and represents to Producer: (a) that all music created, adapted and licensed hereunder is either original or is in the 'public domain' free for use by Producer; (b) that the use of the Music and Master will not infringe upon any rights of any person or entity; (c) that Composer has the right to enter into this Agreement and to grant the Music, and (d) the Master shall not require additional payments to any third parties not described in the Agreement. Composer shall defend, indemnify and hold Producer harmless from any and all costs, losses, damages or expenses arising out of any breach of the foregoing warranties and representations. Composer hereby agrees to indemnify, defend and hold Producer and those authorized by Producer to broadcast the Program harmless from and against any and all claims, damages, costs, liabilities and expenses, including reasonable counsel fees, arising out of the use of the Score as contemplated hereunder. In no event shall the total liability of the Composer hereunder or otherwise exceed the consideration received by Composer hereunder.

4. Producer shall have the right in perpetuity to use the Master and shall retain all right, title and interest, excluding underlying copyright, in and to the Master hereunder as embodied in this production. The results and proceeds of Composer's services hereunder, i.e., the Master, shall be deemed 'works made for hire' (as that term is defined under U.S. Copyright Law). Producer's rights to the Master shall include, but not be limited to, the perpetual, exclusive right to use the Master, or any portion thereof, for any purpose, by any and all means, and in any and all media, whether now known or

hereafter devised, throughout the world in context with the film. Composer maintains ownership of underlying copyright and can use the music in a non-competitive use one (1) year after exhibition. Composer has the right to release the entire score independently subject to the terms of this Agreement.

5. Producer will provide cue sheets for the Music to ASCAP, BMI or any other applicable public performance rights society. Composer will retain ownership of the underlying copyrights, including a 100% control of the Publishing and Writer's royalties. Composer shall be given a copy of the cue sheets filed with the appropriate performing rights society.

6. Composer acknowledges that any exploitation of the Master is at the discretion of Producer and that any revenue generated from the exploitation of the Master pursuant to the rights granted under this Agreement shall belong to Composer.

7. Producer will provide the following credit:
Music Composed by _____
In addition, Composer will receive an equal credit on any print advertising, promotions, DVDs and Videos, wherever other crew members (i.e., cinematographer, editor, co-producer, etc.) receive similar credit.

8. Composer will be given __ copies of the film on both DVD and video after the film is completed.

9. Producer, upon reasonable request, will grant Composer the right to use video and/or still images from the '_____' production for the marketing and promotion of Composer's works, including the Music.

10. This Agreement shall be construed in accordance with the laws of the State of California applicable to agreements entered into and wholly performed therein, as well as any applicable provisions of the U.S. Copyright Law.

11. This Agreement contains the entire understanding of the parties with respect to the subject matter hereof. None of its provisions may be deleted, amended, waived or otherwise modified in the absence of a written document signed by both parties hereto.

'Producer'

_____

By:

'Composer'

By: _____

Ss#_____ Society: _____

- -

One last note about hiring a composer: make sure you are aware of whether all the musicians they bring in to create the score are union or non-union musicians. This is especially important with orchestral scores. If your composer uses union musicians, this means that reuse fees may need to be paid by the broadcaster or exhibitor of your film, and most certainly reuse fees will need to be paid should the score be used by any other company or in any other project. The fees depend on how many union musicians collaborated on the music, so orchestral scores can mean thousands of dollars in reuse royalties. This is why many composers fly to Budapest and Prague to record their scores: because the music isn't recorded in the United States, the musicians will not be American Federation of Musicians members, and, additionally, they are able to use very high-level musicians at a much lower cost.

PRODUCTION MUSIC LIBRARIES

Production music libraries are another good source of music. These are basically online libraries of music where both the publishing and master rights are held by one company. A lot of this music is what they call 'royalty-free,' meaning that no up-front license fee is necessary to use the music in your production. The user of the music receives permission and a license for the use of the music in perpetuity, generally. The library makes income if and when the production is publicly performed (on television, in foreign theaters or over the Internet), but this is not something the content creator is paying for.

INTERNET Per Needledrop	Per Needledrop	30 Min. or Less Blanket	60 Min. Blanket
Broad Internet Rights—Unlimited URLs, including Social Media	$ 500.00	$ 1,800.00	N/A
Limited Internet Streaming Rights—1 URL, excluding Social Media	$ 300.00	$ 900.00	N/A
Each Additional URL	$ 250.00	$ 900.00	N/A
Intranet/Closed Circuit (Internal Company Only)	$ 100.00		N/A
Internet Banner—1 year	$ 300.00	$ 700.00	N/A

COMMERCIAL

Unlimited Tag Packages Per Version/Cut Down	All Media	All Broadcast	Internet	Theatrical	Radio
Worldwide, 1 year	$ 5,300.00	$ 4,700.00	$ 1,250.00	$ 3,750.00	$ 3,400.00
U.S., 1 year	$ 3,700.00	$ 3,000.00	NA	$ 3,750.00	$ 2,000.00
U.S., 13 weeks	$ 2,700.00	$ 2,200.00	NA	$ 1,000.00	$ 1,485.00
Regional, 1 year	$ 1,500.00	$ 1,250.00	NA	$ 900.00	$ 900.00
Local, 1 year	$ 700.00	$ 600.00	NA	$ 500.00	$ 400.00
PSA, 1 year	$ 700.00	$ 600.00	$ 200.00	$ 500.00	$ 400.00
In Store/Kiosk SEE BELOW	NA	NA	NA	NA	NA

Single Commercial Spot Per Needledrop	All Media	All Broadcast	Internet	Theatrical	Radio
Worldwide, Unlimited Package	$ 3,000.00	$ 1,300.00	$ 500.00	$ 1,500.00	$ 750.00
Worldwide, All Media, 1 yr.					
U.S. Unlimited Run, All Media, 1 yr.	$ 1,800.00	$ 950.00	NA	$ 1,000.00	$ 375.00
U.S. 13 weeks, All Media, 1yr.	$ 1,200.00	$ 575.00	NA	$ 750.00	$ 250.00
Regional	$ 900.00	$ 425.00	NA	$ 500.00	$ 165.00
Local	$ 450.00	$ 225.00	NA	$ 500.00	$ 100.00
PSA	$ 350.00	$ 200.00	$ 300.00	$ 500.00	$ 100.00

In Store/Kiosk (Per Needledrop)— One Commercial Spot for 1 year	Unlimited Stores	1,000 Stores	Less Than 1,000 Stores
Worldwide—Airing nationally in any country and/or outside of the U.S.	$ 3,000.00	$ 1,500.00	$ 750.00
National—Airing in the U.S. & Canada in either 2 major markets or more than 5 states	$ 1,500.00	$ 750.00	$ 500.00

Regional—Airing in one major market or up to 5 states		$	500.00	$	300.00
Local—Airing in one state only, no major markets		$	300.00	$	225.00

Live Events—Theaters, Stadiums/Jumbotron, Theme Parks, Hotels, Restaurants	Per Needledrop	30 Min. or Less Blanket
Up to 500 Audience for 1 year	$ 125.00	$ 875.00
Up to 10,000 Audience for 1 year	$ 350.00	$ 1,900.00
Up to 100,000 Audience for 1 year	$ 600.00	$ 3,500.00

Commercials Rights: Definitions

WORLDWIDE: Airing nationally in any country outside of the United States & Canada.
NATIONAL: Airing in the USA & Canada, in either 2 major markets or more than 5 states.
REGIONAL: Airing in 1 major market or up to (and including) 5 states.
LOCAL: Airing in 1 state only. No major markets.
MAJOR MARKETS: New York, Los Angeles, Chicago, Philadelphia, Dallas-Ft Worth, San Francisco-Oakland-San Jose, Boston, Atlanta. Washington DC, Houston
TAGS: Changes to the segment of the original version of the commercial. Tags are ½ the rate of the initial spot. See also tag package pricing.
ALL MEDIA: Free TV, Cable TV, Internet Radio, Satellite Radio, In Theater, Mobile Media, In Store Advertising
ALL BROADCAST: Free TV, Cable, TV, Radio, Satellite Radio
FREE TV: Network/Syndicated
CABLE/SATELLITE TV: Basic & Premium, DBS and Pay-Per-View
INTERNET: Worldwide, Unlimited Views/Hits
RADIO: Network/Syndicated, Satellite Transmission
IN THEATER: Movie Theaters or other public venues
**RATES DO NOT INCLUDE CAMPAIGNS

Figure 5.5 Generic music library rate card

Using music from a production music library is easy since it is 'one-stop,' which means that the publishing and master rights are included in the price. Some are niche-specific, such as Seven Seas Music, which focuses on authentic international music, and Marmoset, which focuses on indie rock bands. Others have many genres of music, such as Extreme Music, APM, FirstCom, and Manhattan Music. The price of a song from one of these companies is generally less than that of major labels and publishers, and probably the best part is the turn-around time, which is instantaneous if not within 24 hours. These platforms exist to make the work of the media producers swifter. It is generally easy to search, listen and license music. There is a rate card that the 'buyer' can request and reference to find the price of a track. The rate card will look something like that shown in Figure 5.5.

These prices, however, are not always set in stone, especially if a production decides to license more than one track. Licensing multiple tracks is called 'bundling.' It is done frequently to lower the price of individual tracks, and provides more revenue to the library.

Libraries were conceived years before the advent of television. It was during the era of radio, when stations would hire live bands to play music behind spoken-word shows. These musicians employed by the radio stations would play the intro and outro of shows, as well as playing during the break. Music used for a transition to a break is called 'bump' music or 'bumper' music. The music was often thematic, to give the program a unique and memorable sound.

The networks established the ABC radio band and CBS band to record music and use it over and again on various shows. It probably diluted the live musicians' work, but led to greater ease of use and strengthened the networks' music library.

To this day, television and cable networks contract music libraries on an annual, or blanket, basis so their producers have a plethora of music to choose from. Producers and editors can access the music at a post house or office since most of these libraries are available digitally. Downloading and watermarking the music facilitates more accurate music logs. These music logs, commonly called cue sheets, are used for reporting purposes by networks to the publishers and their collection agencies.

"There are so many libraries now," comments Manhattan Production Music Library VP Ron Goldberg.

> There are new ones coming up every week. Even composers have libraries. We have the Chesky brand, which is not stock music. It's a label and we believe in it. It's not the quick, synthesized cues that you hear in most libraries.

"Rates have not gone up because many production budgets have gone down," continues Goldberg. "Competitors don't seem to care about quality and price. They are not charging the right price for certain uses and this kills the business. To compete against so many libraries, we must come up with other ideas." For Manhattan it is their focus on indie artists and great cues.

Almost all the major labels have a leg in the music production library business—Warner/Chappell Production Music has been in business for 35 years. Some purchased production libraries instead of creating their own (such as Sony/ATV, which purchased Extreme Music in the early 2010s), and many took their lower-hanging fruit and created cues from their own stash of music. Libraries usually get their content by commissioning composers to write original works for them or by signing artists who will license pre-recorded music to them. Original works are generally commissioned for a flat fee as a work-for-hire, and the original composer sometimes retains his right to collect public performance royalties, but not always. Where the music is licensed and pre-recorded, the composer and the library usually split third-party licensing income on a 50/50 basis. Of course, these points are negotiable, but on average these are the common ways content is obtained for library use.

In sum, music libraries are a great resource for finding quality, quick music cues that one can license remotely. Most offer easy online systems that allow you to search, download, automatically generate a license, pay and be on your merry way.

Also, many production companies, such as we had at ESPN, secure an annual license so that all their producers, editors and the like can access the wealth of music in each library and not report each and every one when used. A standard 'blanket' license is created and then the track's details are reported on a cue sheet which is delivered to the library at the end of the year. The library can then assess the amount used and see if they want to increase their rate the next year. A reduction of rate only generally occurs if less of the library content is needed. Either way, the library enjoys the ability to have a long-standing relationship with the networks and production houses and the user has free rein to use whatever tracks they like.

Here is a sample annual license agreement:

ANNUAL LICENSE AGREEMENT

Agreement made between Lovely Production Music, at Lovely Offices, 333 Loving Street, New York, NY 10000 (herein referred to as 'Publisher') and We are the Real Sports Network, having offices at 20 Guest Street, Boston, MA, 02000 (herein referred to as 'Licensee') as follows:

I. GRANT OF RIGHTS

For good and valuable consideration which the parties hereby acknowledge, Publisher hereby grants to Licensee, first, a retroactive license for all previous videos produced by Lennar Homes with the song 'Time of Your Life' by Paul Suchow. In addition, Publisher will also provide to Licensee the following rights to selected musical compositions herein defined as unlimited downloads of the entire Apple Trax (1–151), Live Trax (1–80), All Media Music (101–171), BRg (1001–4042) and Empire Trailer Series (1–6) libraries plus updates as they become available (Publisher's Library) for three years commencing on November 1, 2016 and terminating on October 31, 2019 as follows:

A. The non-exclusive license to record and re-record (without limitation to the number of uses) the recorded musical selections in Publisher's Library for the sole and limited purpose of including and reproducing same in a sound track for use only in connection with Internet, broadcast or non-broadcast programming produced solely by Licensee.

B. TERRITORY: The territory covered by this agreement is **the World**.

C. EXPIRATION OF TERM: Upon the termination of this agreement, Licensee shall be precluded from releasing any new, previously unreleased productions featuring the Music. In addition, at Licensee's expense electronically erase all the recorded musical selections described herein unless both parties agree to a new agreement to license Publisher's Libraries. Termination of this Agreement resulting from any breach thereof by Licensee or for any other reason, other than breach thereof by Publisher, shall not relieve Licensee of its obligation to pay the full License Fee (as hereinafter defined) or any portion thereof still due to Publisher at the time of termination. This clause is of the essence of this Agreement. All other previously released productions using the Publisher's content can continue to be in the marketplace in perpetuity, provided that such productions are not edited or altered in any shape or form.

D. With prior written permission from the Licensee, the Publisher has permission to, from time to time; display a production that Licensee has produced that utilized the recorded musical selections, on the Publisher's website for promotional purposes only [the 'Promotional Display']. If necessary, Licensee agrees to provide Publisher with any copyright or other permissions language that Licensee would like the Publisher to include in such Promotional Display. The permission granted by you herein does not include or permit Publisher to sublicense the Promotional Display to any third parties whatsoever without prior written permission.

II. LIMITATION OF RIGHTS

A. This license is not assignable or transferable by Licensee by operation of law or otherwise.

B. This license is limited to Licensee, and includes Licensee's subsidiaries, parent company, affiliates, and partners.

C. This license does not authorize the public performance of the recorded musical selections by means of theatrical exhibition to the general public, except as set forth above.

D. It is understood and agreed by the Licensee that it hereby acquires no rights in or to the Publisher's Library and that the Publisher's Library remains the sole and exclusive property of the Publisher. Publisher in its sole and absolute discretion may, at any time during the term of this agreement, remove Licensee's access to downloading Publisher's Library.
E. Licensee hereby agrees that the Publisher's Library is a unique and valuable property of the Publisher. Licensee hereby agrees and acknowledges that any unauthorized use will cause irreparable harm to the Publisher and that the Publisher shall be entitled to immediate injunctive relief.
F. Licensee shall pay to the Publisher reasonable attorneys' fees and expenses necessarily incurred by the Publisher in order to enforce any of the provisions of this agreement.
G. This license does not authorize broadcasting, cablecasting, or the public performance of the recorded musical selections other than as expressly authorized herein.

III. LICENSE FEE

In consideration of the license granted herein, Licensee agrees to pay the Publisher a license fee in the amount of **$10,000 (Ten Thousand Dollars) per year for 1 year.** This license is valid only upon receipt by Lovely Production Music of a signed and dated copy of said license along with payment.

IV. WARRANTIES AND REPRESENTATIONS

A. The Publisher represents and warrants that it has full power and authority to enter into this agreement and grant the rights granted herein. Publisher shall indemnify and hold harmless the Licensee and all parties identified under section IIB from and against any and all losses, liabilities, claims, costs, damages and expenses, including attorneys' fees and court costs arising out of or resulting from any third-party claims related to the Publisher's breach of or alleged breach of any representation or warranty made by Publisher under this section IV.

B. ASCAP/BMI AND PERFORMING RIGHTS

1. The Publisher represents and warrants that all of the musical compositions contained in the Publisher's Library are contained in the ASCAP/BMI repertoire.
2. Licensee shall include in all agreements for the television or radio exhibition of any programming produced here under which utilizes the Publisher's Library, a term and condition that said television station, radio station, cable or satellite entity shall comply with the reporting provisions of their ASCAP/BMI license agreement.

V. BREACH OR DEFAULT

Upon any breach or default by Licensee of any term or condition herein the Publisher may terminate this agreement upon notice to the Licensee. Licensee shall then promptly return any property owned and provided by the Publisher and the Licensee shall promptly pay all fees due under the terms of this agreement.

VI. NOTICE

All notices required or permitted hereunder shall be given in writing by certified mail sent to either party at the address stated herein. Each party agrees to inform the other of any change of address.

VII. RESERVATION OF RIGHTS

All rights not specifically granted herein are reserved by the Publisher.

VIII. STATE LAW

This agreement and all of the terms and conditions herein shall be governed and construed in accordance with the laws of the State of New York. Licensee hereby agrees that a court of competent jurisdiction within the State of New York, County of New York, shall have jurisdiction over this agreement. If any clause, sentence, paragraph or portion of this agreement, or the application thereof, shall be found to be invalid by a court of competent jurisdiction, the remainder of the agreement shall survive.

IN WITNESS WHEREOF, this agreement is executed by the Licensee this 9/18/15.

WE ARE THE REAL SPORTS NETWORK	**LOVELY PRODUCTION MUSIC**
LICENSEE	
Signed:_____	Signed: _____
Print: _____	Print:_____
Title:_____	Title:_____

- -

COMMERCIAL MUSIC

Another popular method is, of course, the licensing of commercial music. This tends to be the most expensive method, simply because separate rights must be secured from the publishing company and from the recording company. Commercial music is music that has been previously released and is available to purchase via retail. Since these recordings are generally by musical artists who make a living from their trade, the songwriter could be different from the recording artist, and permission must be granted from both parties. This takes time and there is protocol involved; it is more onerous and pricey. The licensing process is covered in depth in Chapter 6.

Using previously recorded music costs the most because of all the entities involved and the songs' varying popularity. Some songs are under pre-existing **exclusivity** deals that may inhibit another media producer's ability to use the song. For example, George Gershwin's "Rhapsody in Blue" has been used by United Airlines for their safety video and brand recognition; hence, it cannot be used by another airline for a set amount of time. Since a film is a different media platform, and one that would not interfere with the United use, this does not deter a filmmaker from using it, however.

Commercial music is also needed when a specific scene is shot during, or references, a particular historic time and place. Music supervisors can help locate commercial music for this use. Their job is to source music within a filmmaker's budget quickly and with all the necessary rights secured.

DISCOVERY

There are many places to discover music for your production if you are not keen to employ a composer or use music production libraries. However, wherever you discover this music, you will need to make sure you can get the rights cleared. There are some music discovery sites that can secure the rights from their site, and others cannot.

Many producers turn to YouTube to source music, but that can be a dangerous pit since no (reliable) information about where the source of the music is coming from exists. In order to incorporate music, you must be granted permission by the copyright holders and if you can't find their information, then you will have an issue.

Bandcamp, Beatport and SoundCloud are great discovery sites as well, where many times there are links to contact the artist directly. It can sometimes be frustrating, however, since artists don't always respond in a timely fashion.

Another source of music, especially used by students and those seeking free music, is the **Creative Commons** site. This is a website where artists have hosted their music to be heard and potentially used by media producers. These artists have signed a release that allows other creative individuals to use their music for free, with certain pre-selected limitations. If, for example, you are using a song in another creative work (e.g., sampling the song in a new composition) the use may be free. Yet if you are planning to use the song in a streaming advertisement, there may be a fee. What is lovely about Creative Commons is that the creators of the music have put their own restrictions on each sort of media use. It is truly user-based, thanks to copyright lawyer and founder Lawrence Lessig.

Most musicians relish the opportunity to work with media creators. It's exciting to collaborate and it's equally exciting when a filmmaker or television producer licenses a piece of music to use in their production. Unbeknownst to the filmmaker, the use of music in a production can generate additional monies for the artist, which has become a necessity in today's world. The use of music in television and in theaters outside the United States can generate residual income royalties through a show's re-airing.

This residual income is known as a performance royalty from any public performance of a song. It is only afforded to composers and writers of music. In order to receive this money, composers must join a performing rights organization. In the United States they should sign up as a writer with one of the three performing rights societies—ASCAP, BMI or SESAC—and then register each song. Each song must have a contact or publishing company associated with it in order for the monies to be paid out. This information is very important for the composer; it is crucial for the media producer. The only time a filmmaker needs to be attentive to the proper information is when filling out a cue sheet, but the composer or publishers should provide the production company with accurate information to list. Armed with this reporting, these performing rights organizations, who act essentially as collection agencies, will then collect any income from the public performance of the music in the production for their writers. This comes predominately from television and radio use, and more recently streaming use.

Licensing music into a production, whether a previously-used score or commercial pop song, can generate significant revenue for an artist and songwriter. Once a song is placed in a production money is generated by the synchronization fee and often times there are additional royalties garnered for the songwriter through public performance. These monies are not paid out by the filmmaker, TV producer or new media producer. They are paid out by the media station itself (television network, website hosting company, or, outside the United States, theaters). Any public performance space will pay for the use of commercial music. Examples of this are hair salons, bars, TV stations, corporate offices and facilities (like retail stores or large grocery chains). It is important to remember that the media producer does not pay this additional royalty; the broadcasting entity does.

One other source of creative music ideas is through new digital search engine platforms, which are music companies with websites from which users can search a catalog for their music needs. These websites represent music that is either available for license immediately via a rate card, or within a day or two. They generally have pre-recorded original music and are ready to license quickly. Some of these sites offer a service to compose a piece of music within a day upon getting details about the pitch, and others simply send along music to satisfy the music request. All-in-all they are a sort of hybrid between a music library and a **song plugger**, someone who represents a music catalog for placement into film and TV.

There is so much music content with so many opportunities. Senior Creative Director Andre Comeau for Seven Seas Music says,

> It can be daunting to locate the best avenue for music. There is an over-saturation of music, so niche offerings are becoming more important. A lot of productions are using international locations, and using world music legitimizes a particular scene. It is very necessary. Frankly it is one of the underutilized areas of the licensing world, and there so much music and so much possibility. It is exciting to be a part of it. I do see that as a very positive trend.

Music is plentiful. There are hundreds of thousands of outlets from which to source great sound for your project. Content is everywhere you look— and if you are reading this book, then it's safe to assume your creative network boasts a friend or family member that could compose an original song for you at little to no cost. This is a great option if you are working on a student film or have a minimal budget to work from. So are libraries and royalty-free music sources. The decision to hire a composer or license commercial music is usually one that rests on budget (how much can you spend), creativity (does the scene call for a particular piece of music), and time (as a composer takes time to compose, and a license takes time to procure). The best advice would be to think 'big picture.' Think of the overall project, what you must have and what you can live without. Perhaps you buy any old techno beat for the club scene in Act One, but you shell out for the Springsteen song that your character can't get around without singing to in the car in Act Two. These considerations are daunting, especially when a lot of music cues are used in your project—which is where a music supervisor can really help.

6

THE PROCESS OF SECURING RIGHTS

A Step-by-Step Guide to Avoiding Mistakes, Because What You Don't Know Can Cost You

The process of securing music rights can be a daunting task. The most important aspect about clearing music is knowing, and truly understanding, that there are two copyrights to be secured. There is the permission from the writer(s) of the song, secured through the publisher; and there is the permission of the performer or artist who realized or recorded the song, secured through the owner of the master—usually the record label.

Unlike other forms of art where there is generally only one copyright holder involved, music has two creators, hence two copyright holders. There is the individual(s) who wrote the song—called the songwriter, composer or lyricist—and there is the artist who performs the song—called the performer or recording artist. Sometimes they are the same person and many times they are not. For example, the song "Nothing Compares 2 U" made famous by poet-songstress Sinead O'Connor was written by Prince, not Sinead O'Connor. So if you were to use this recorded version of the song in your production, you would need to secure permission from Prince Rogers Nelson (the songwriter's legal name) through his publisher, Controversy Music c/o Universal Music Publishing, and permission from Sinead O'Connor (the artist) through her record label, Chrysalis Records.

Then, let's say you wanted to use Prince's recorded version instead. You would still need to get permission from his publisher, Universal Music Publishing, for use of the composition, and then obtain permission from his record label, Warner Music. This is a rather simple example, but as you can see, Warner and Chrysalis are different business entities, so it is very important to know where you are headed in order to secure the rights from the correct entity. Many songs have multiple writers and therefore you must get permission from all the writers through all the publishers in order to use the song.

An example of this sort of research is exemplified in the song "California Gurls" performed by Katy Perry. The composition was written by eight individuals and those eight writers are represented by six publishers. All six publishers would need to be contacted if you wanted to use this song. Here are the details:

Writers	Publishers
Calvin Cordazor Broadus—BMI	Kobalt Music
Lukasz Gottwald—ASCAP	Warner Chappell Music
Katheryn Elizabeth Hudson—ASCAP	Matza Ball Music
Benjamin Joseph Levin—N/A	EMI
Michael Edward Love—N/A	Songs of Pulse Recording
Max Martin—STIM	Universal
Bonnie Leigh McKee—BMI	
Brian Douglas Wilson—BMI	

The first step to **clearing** music—the process of granting or obtaining permission to use the song in a production—is to identify the copyright holders of the song you want to use. It's not always clear and requires research to get it right.

For example, let's say you are looking to clear "Always on My Mind," popularly recorded by the artist Willie Nelson. A search on the ASCAP website lists 170 titles by this name, while the BMI website lists 211. Instead of sifting through all these results to find the right one, a simple search on Wikipedia would reveal that this classic love song was written by Johnny Christopher, Mark James and Wayne Carson. Having both the writer and performer information is a tremendous help in drilling down and finding the exact title you need, and getting the appropriate publisher information to clear the right song.

Also, one has to be careful about songs in the public domain. This means the song has fallen out of copyright protection. Yet in some cases a writer could take a public-domain song and create their own new arrangement of the song and publish that arrangement. For example, if you are interested in using the song "Take Me Out to the Ball Game" and start a copyright search, you will discover that there are multiple copyright registrations due to the fact that many people have copyrighted their arrangement of the song. The song is really in the public domain, so in doing your search you may have located various arrangements. If you have friends sing the song for your production then you are using the public-domain version, but if you decide to use a recorded version for your film, look into which version you are using since you will need to be granted permission for that particular arranged recording.

Once you have located the accurate information about the writer and performer, the process of requesting a license, or permission, begins. There is protocol involved and in today's world all is done through email. Documentation of when a request was sent and what rights are being requested exactly are all very pertinent to substantiating your request. Most requests look like this:

Date
Publisher
Address

Re: Synch Use of "Feel Right" in a Short Series Entitled *The Operatives*

Dear Publisher:

In *The Operatives*, the series opens in a highly classified location where four brilliant grad students are interrogated by government operatives. Why? Because the world is about to end, and it's all their fault. After using cutting-edge science for their own petty purposes, this ragtag team creates a small but potentially world-ending black hole in their college lab. The solution? Tell the government EVERY illegal thing they've done in the lab. This series is for digital media distribution only. There are six episodes in total, which each run 22–30 minutes each.

Episode Budget: $400,000 USD
Total Songs: 1 song
Series Distributor: Rooster Teeth

We would like to request your permission for the following use(s):

- Title: "Feel Right";
- Writers: Thomas Brenneck, Christopher Brown, Peter Hernandez, Philip Lawrence, Nick Movshon, Mark Ronson, Home Steinweiss;
- Usage(s); Timing(s): Background vocal; Up to full use of song;
- Scene Description: Episode 4—Heard over the funniest montage of entire series where main characters build their business, and over dream sequence;
- Rights Requested: All digital media rights including mobile, worldwide, in perpetuity;
- MFN: With all songs;
- Option: (a) limited theatrical, U.S., 6 months; and (b) cable TV, U.S., 3 years.

Please contact me should you foresee any problems with this request.

Thank you,
Supervisor

———————————

- -

The request includes the date, production company (and brief description thereof) and two to three sentences about the project; plus the song title, writer or performer (depending on who you are sending the request to); duration of the use of music; term you intend to use the song for (one year, five years, perpetuity, etc.); and use (which defines whether the song is being used as a visual vocal, visual instrumental, background instrumental or background vocal, or theme music). In many cases, it addresses MFN, or 'most favored nations' (a concept which basically ensures, in this case, that the most favorable compensation being offered to any song holder will be offered to this publisher). It also includes the most important factor: the media of exhibition being licensed. 'Media' is a very broad term. Here is a list of some media descriptions:

- "Film Festival Exhibition";
- "Educational Exhibition";
- "Art-House Theatrical Exhibition" or "Limited Theatrical Exhibition";
- "Motion Picture Theatrical Exhibition";
- "Non-Theatrical Exhibition" or "Corporate Use";
- "All Television Media";
- "Free TV";
- "Basic Cable TV";
- "Pay/Pay-Per-View/Video-On-Demand/Subscription TV";
- "Home Video/DVD";
- "Videogram(s)";
- "Internet Streaming";

- "Digital Download";
- "All Digital Media";
- "All New Media."

There are things to be aware of when requesting the use of music in your production:

1. Don't give out too much information. This can be a deterrent. The licensor may come back with more questions, so make it simple and easy for them to understand.
2. Don't follow up with phone calls. Send emails.
3. They may ask for the project's overall budget and base the fee on that. Be accurate within reason. Some may even ask for your 'music budget.' You can provide if one is available. For example: "Film budget: $8M; Music Budget: $250,000."
4. Make sure the individual you are securing the music from is in fact the actual owner (or controller) of the copyright and will give your production **indemnity**. Indemnity is a promise to defend you in court if a third party sues you for copyright infringement. There are some situations where a music producer grants approval for a song, but they are not fully authorized to do so. We had an encounter with a producer who had the artist Common perform a rap on a song, and the producer granted us the rights to use the song, stating that he controlled both the master and publishing, when in fact Common had a portion of the writer's share. To rectify this, one has to paddle backward and re-negotiate the licensing fee and have all the licenses re-issued. It was not fun.

RESEARCH TOOLS

There are a few sources to help you locate the proper writers and their publishers. The most commonly used are the performing rights organizations that represent writers and publishers and collect public performance monies for each of them from broadcasters and online platforms. Every country outside the United States has only one. However, in the United States we have three—ASCAP (American Society of Composers, Authors and Publishers), BMI (Broadcast Music Incorporated) and SESAC (Society of European Stage Authors and Composers). Each site allows you to search by artist, song title, songwriter/composer or publisher.

allmusic.com

This is a great website for locating an album's date of release and label information. This site allows you to search a song by artist, title or album title. Be careful and always look for the earliest version of the recording because that will show the original release date and label, which is the first owner of the recording in question. It will be the original record label that released the song, which is generally what you want. What the site does not always show are the writers of the song. They do a pretty good job, but searching via ASCAP, BMI and SESAC is more accurate.

What All Music Guide does glean is the birth name of the artist. So, for example, if you are looking up the band Animal Collective, you may not see the names of the writers, but if you read the bio, it will probably tell you. "Animal Collective were formed in Baltimore County, Maryland, by longtime friends and musical collaborators Avery Tar (David Portner), Panda Bear (Noah Lennox), Deakin (Josh Dibb) and Geologist (Brian Weitz)." Then, if you were to look up the writer(s) of a particular Animal Collective song, you will have their legal names and it will be easier to locate the publisher information.

harryfox.com

Harry Fox is another good source for locating writer and publisher information. In order to discover publisher information, you must go to www.harryfox.com and search under 'Songfile' and then do a 'public search.' You must accept its terms and then you can search by song title and writer. If you don't have any writer information, the title will suffice, but it must be spelled properly!

pdinfo.com

This is a public-domain information website to visit if you want to look up songs in the public domain, or search to see if a song is in the public domain.

IMDB.com

The Internet Movie Database is a good place to find any information relating to a film release, including composers and soundtracks. Some find it helpful to search for music-related information here. It's especially useful when one knows the film the song is from or where one heard it, but that's about it.

Getting all your information correct is the best start you can have. Spelling accuracy and copyright holder knowledge is the foundation for any music rights negotiation. All this detail is also necessary for later when filling out the cue sheet.

CUE SHEET

The cue sheet is a log of the music (**cues**) in the exact order in which each piece was heard in the production. These are very important documents which are filled out by the director, editor, composer or music editor, and supplemented by information provided by the music supervisor. They require a lot of detail and must be completed with accuracy, especially using proper spelling. A spelling mistake could affect a composer's or writer's receipt of pay. In a cue sheet, the 'use' provides information about the way in which the song was used, e.g., TH = theme or main theme, BV = background vocal, VV = visual vocal (when someone is singing on stage in a show).

Other information needed to complete the cue sheet is exact timing of the use of the song, or cue, and the precise writer and publisher information. Cue sheets are completed once a production is locked and are generally part of the delivery requirements before a TV show airs or film is delivered to the distributor. Most importantly, these cue sheets contain the proper performing rights (ASCAP, BMI, SESAC, GEMA, PRS, etc.) information and percentages. This information can be found on the individual music licenses once secured.

Here is an example of a cue sheet:

"Fun Production" MUSIC CUE SHEET

Film/Series/Ep Title and #:			Distributor:				
Director:	Mr Fun		Production Company: By The Beach Productions, Inc			Release Territory: world	
Release Date:			Address: Los Angeles, CA				
Program Length:	58m 06 se		Phone: Total Music Duration:				
Program Type: FILM / SERIES /	DOCUMENTARY						

CUE #	CUE/SONG TITLE	COMPOSER(S)	PRO	%	PUBLISHER(S)	PRO	%	TIME	USAGE
1	Company Logo ID	Lon Bender	ASCAP	50%	Maisie Anthems	ASCAP	50%	:04	Logo
		Charlie Campagna	BMI	50%	Maisie Beats	BMI	50%		
2	Konec = End	Yuri Tomanek	APRA	100%	self published	NA	100%	4:52	BI
3	68	Gabriel Garzon-Montano	BMI	100%	Downtown DMP Songs	BMI	100%	1:52	BV
4	Sleep Is the Most	Yuri Tomanek	APRA	100%	Maisie Anthems	ASCAP	100%	1:00	BI
5	To Market	Christopher Todd Griffin	BMI	100%	Christopher Todd Griffin	BMI	100%	1:10	BI
6	What's Happened to Me?	Yuri Tomanek	APRA	100%	Maisie Anthems	ASCAP	100%	1:25	BI
7	Probably the Best Part of Me	Yuri Tomanek	APRA	100%	Maisie Anthems	ASCAP	100%	:40	BI
8	Totally Optimistic	Christopher Todd Griffin	BMI	100%	Christopher Todd Griffin	BMI	100%	1:02	BI
13	Moonbeams	Adam Hurlburt	ASCAP	50%	Amateur Music	ASCAP	100%	2:22	BI
		Joshua Scott	ASCAP	50%					
14	Spice Mon	James Drew Casella	ASCAP	100%	Tapspace Publications	ASCAP	100%	1:50	VI, BI
15	Down In Mississippi	Traditional	NA	100%	NA			1:00	BV
16	Company Logo ID	Lon Bender	ASCAP	50%	Maisie Anthems	ASCAP	50%	:04	BI
		Charlie Campagna	BMI	50%	Maisie Beats	BMI	50%		

*Use Codes for Usage Field: MT = Main Title   ET = End Title   BI = Background Instrumental   VI = Visual Instrumental
BV = Background Vocal   VV = Visual Vocal
**Use Codes for Music Origin Field: Commissioned   Licensed   Music Library License

Since the cue sheet is created to pay authors of music for the public performance of their songs, cue sheets are not required for straight-to-video DVDs or video games. They are obligatory for any show aired on TV or in theaters, streamed on the web, or broadcast over the radio.

After the request for use has been submitted, there is the waiting period. This can take from a few days to a few months, all depending on, for example, the time it takes for the copyright holder to contact their person of interest. Many times a lower-budget project can take a longer period to get a response, simply because it is lower on the totem pole. If an artist is on tour or in the studio, many times it is hard to get a response quickly.

Generally, a response is positive, and with that approval right a quote is provided as well. Yet some times you receive a **denial**. This is a term used when the copyright holder says "No" to your use. This is generally given for two reasons. The first is they don't like your budget. Requesting Aerosmith's song "Back in the Saddle" for a documentary with a $200,000 budget, which can only spend $5,000 on this song, did not fly. The label responded by saying this song reaped over $250,000 for films. In this case, bye-bye song.

The second reason for a denial is generally given when the songwriter or artist does not like the subject matter, or the way a song will be used in a film. In one documentary about a religious figure who had recently spent time in jail and was now back on the circuit, the scene showed him coming onto a stage while using a hit song to energize the crowd. The song was denied.

One of the more unusual, yet validated, cases encountered was the attempt of a filmmaker to use two minutes of the Mavis Staples version of the song "Eye on the Prize." The filmmaker requested to use this song as a backdrop to images of a very right-wing reverend who returns to his hometown of Buffalo, New York. The song plays as he drives his car and recalls the pro-life protests he participated in. Archival footage of these protests, including shots of him as a younger man, were interspersed with images of the present day. Management felt the song was being used to create as much power as its original intended use, where it represented black strength and struggle during the Civil Rights movement. This was not the case in this specific use, and secondly, the reverend was carrying a black fetus, which of course did not sit well with the artist. These sorts of underlying issues, or contextual placements, are what can easily bring denials.

In a request there are other pieces of relevant information that need to be addressed. These are:

Term

The length of time you plan to use the piece of music in your production. Most distributors would like you to get perpetuity rights, which means they can use the piece of music, as it is heard in the production, forever. However, many copyright holders are now limiting the rights to five, seven or ten years. This means that at the end of the term you will need to re-negotiate these terms. This situation is not ideal. However, reducing the term can reduce the price.

Territory

This is the territory in which you need your production to be cleared for use. Generally, it is the world or universe. In some cases, like an advertisement, the rights may only need to be secured for the United States or for a particular region, state or country. Reducing the territory, if possible, will reduce the cost as well. These days, however, almost all media is being streamed on the web. If that is the case, then a "worldwide" right needs to be secured.

Use

This is how the song is being heard in the production. Is it being heard in the background, or as an instrumental, or as the main theme, or as a "teaser," which is the trailer or marketing tool to grasp someone's attention. Many times, a short film may use one piece of music to "bed" or soundtrack the entire three-minute movie. Other times, there may be five pieces of music used in one twenty-minute short. All these factors help the licensor better understand how their copyrighted material, or song, is going to be used in your production and helps them better assess the value of your project.

Media

This explanation is the crux of what determines the fee for a piece of music in a production. The "media" explains where the production is going to be exhibited. Today there are so many more media outlets than in the past. Only about a decade ago there was simply (a) theatrical; (b) TV—cable or network; (c) film festival; (d) DVD; and (e) educational. Today we can offer our clients licenses covering many more, which can look like this:

- "Film Festival Exhibition"—The right to exhibit the production to audiences at film festivals and non-marquee theaters.
- "Educational Exhibition"—The right to exhibit the production to audiences (whether or not admission is charged) in educational facilities (i.e., high schools, universities, libraries and museums).
- "Art-House Theatrical Exhibition" or "Limited Theatrical Exhibition"—The right to exhibit the production (whether or not admission is charged) in theaters aimed at small niche-market audiences. These are small capacity theaters. Independent filmmakers will secure art-house theatrical rights, if any.
- "Motion Picture Theatrical Exhibition"—The right to exhibit the production to audiences in theaters, film festivals and other places of public entertainment where motion pictures are customarily exhibited and admission is charged (think mainstream blockbuster movies). These are big-budget films with nationwide ad campaigns. Most independent filmmakers will not need to secure motion picture theatrical rights.
- "Non-Theatrical Exhibition" or "Corporate Use"—The right to exhibit the production to audiences on common carriers such as airlines, trains, ships and buses, as well as in diplomatic installations, military establishments, clubs, bars, restaurants and similar "non-theatrical" venues where there is typically no direct charge for viewing imposed. This method of exhibition is sometimes also referred to as "**corporate use**."
- "All Television Media"—The right to exhibit the production by all forms of television broadcast and/or transmission now known and hereinafter devised, whether such programming is transmitted via wires, wireless, cables, satellite, or any other communication channels, including free, basic cable, pay and subscription television; pay-per-view; and video-on-demand (VOD). This right specifically excludes transmission of the

production that enables the end user to purchase a permanent download or copy of the production, "videograms" or so-called "podcasting."

- "Free TV"—The right to exhibit the production over the facilities of television broadcast networks and local television broadcast stations (not cable transmission or "CATV" transmissions) that furnish such broadcast without charge to the viewer and which are received by and exhibited on a television broadcast receiver or other similar viewing device (e.g., local channels, ABC, CBS, NBC).
- "Basic Cable TV"—The right to exhibit the production by means of cable television systems, whether such programming is transmitted via wire, wireless, cables, satellite or any other communication channels, for which members of the public may pay for the transmission service provided by such cable system (e.g., TNT, ESPN, National Geographic, Sundance Channel). There are many tiers of basic cable. If you know the specific network on which your production will be exhibited, please advise so appropriate television rights are secured.
- "Pay/Pay-Per-View/Video-On-Demand/Subscription TV"—The right to exhibit the production to a television set or other viewing device on which the ultimate viewer receives the broadcast upon the one-time or periodic payment of a subscription fee or premium (e.g., HBO, STARZ, IFC). This right specifically excludes transmission of the production that enables the end user to purchase a permanent download or copy of the production, "videograms" or so-called "podcasting."
- "Home Video/DVD/Blu-Ray"—The right to exhibit the production by means of audio-visual devices that are intended primarily for personal home use (such as digital video discs (DVDs) or Blu-Ray). It does not include digital downloading, VOD, Netflix or other general entertainment streaming platforms.
- "Videogram(s)"—Videogram(s) shall mean and include all audio-visual devices intended for personal, non-commercial exhibition of the production by means of any viewing device whether capable of being viewed or otherwise exhibited by means of any so-called interactive devices or cable systems including but not limited to CD-I, CD-ROM, or any other future storage and/or retrieval devices or systems. Videogram(s) shall

include: Tangible devices such as DVDs and Blu-Ray; and digital distribution (whether wired or wireless) of downloadable video "files" (e.g., available through a music service for reproduction on a portable viewing device), so-called "podcasting," or any other similar technologies or means of distributing a non-ephemeral or permanent download or copy of the production to consumers, e.g., iTunes and Amazon.

- "Internet Streaming"—The right to exhibit the production on your company, official film, or agency website only. This right is limited to streaming (non-downloadable) use, and specifically excludes the right of an end user to download the production (compare with digital download rights, below). If you intend to post your production onto a third-party website (e.g., YouTube), please indicate your intent so that appropriate permission is secured.
- "Digital Download"—The right to exhibit the production in a digital format that allows end users to download the production at cost or otherwise. This right is usually bundled with Internet rights, home video/DVD rights or television rights.
- "All Digital Media"—The right to exhibit the production via electronic and digital devices for individual viewing (such as Internet streaming, digital download, VOD and disc-on-demand) for both digital and physical delivery of the production, whether for exhibition on television, computer, hand-held devices or otherwise. Digital media excludes theatrical exhibition of any kind, television transmission and traditional home video/DVD devices.
- "All New Media"—The right to exhibit the production in any and all new media whether now known or hereinafter devised. As you can imagine, all new media encompasses a whole lot! If your distributor requires that you secure new media rights, please advise so that we can determine the true breadth of the rights you need.
- "In-Context Trailer Use"—The right to exhibit the song as it is heard in the context of the film or production. This is a promotional use, or trailer use, but the song is heard exactly as it is heard within the production. Many times, this use is included, for no additional fee, in the license agreement of a song that is being secured for broad rights.

- "Out-of-Context Trailer Use"—The right to use a song in a trailer which may or may not be in the film or production. This is also a promotional, or trailer, use. Songs used in this nature are typically costlier than within a production because the use is promoting a film. Many times too, the song will not even be in the film. Since it is used in the trailer to promote the film, this license comes under marketing, and many times is not included in a film's overall budget.

INITIAL RIGHTS VS. OPTIONS

Theatrical rights were one of the priciest media configurations to secure, but not anymore. Digital platforms have become the norm. Theatrical configurations are quietly becoming less and less important. Many productions are not being distributed into theaters and are instead being released on digital platforms, so the licensors who once were able to reap additional financial rewards from box office receipts are needing to find other ways to bring in additional revenue.

Knowing exactly how your production is going to be exhibited is what affects the price. Independent filmmakers who are creating a production without knowing their distributor will have to consider where they may think their film will be distributed when securing music rights. If they shoot too broad, they will pay through the nose. If they request too-limited rights, they may have to go back to secure more rights.

A filmmaker secured the music rights for her short documentary. She had four songs licensed, including "New York New York," written by Fred Ebb and John Kander, which was controlled by EMI Music Publishing. The songs were initially cleared for film festival exhibition and DVD release. Shortly after securing these rights, the film was nominated for an Academy Award, and HBO picked it up for television distribution. The supervisor had to go back to the copyright holders and request these rights. Unfortunately for the filmmaker, from the time the film exhibited at film festivals to the time it was picked up by HBO, EMI Music Publishing was sold to Sony/ATV. The new owners of the company felt that "New York New York" was one of their biggest copyright assets and wanted to charge over $10,000 for use of that song alone. Negotiations went on for months until a price was settled that the filmmaker could afford and Sony/ATV could accept. Had she secured all television media rights up-front she would have paid more at the time, but perhaps not as much as she ultimately had to. It is never clear what can transpire when new rights are needed and one has to go back to the drawing board.

Initial rights are the rights you need immediately. They are the rights you need to exhibit your film first. "All media rights in perpetuity" gives the widest range of rights because they are not limiting, and as a result they are the most expensive.

Limiting rights will decrease the price. Therefore, your initial rights are the ones you need out-the-door. Some examples are:

- Film festival rights, worldwide, one year;
- DVD release rights, U.S. only, seven years;
- Educational rights, U.S. only, five years;
- Corporate use rights, U.S. only.

Options are a right that you may need at a later time but will not be paying for up-front. They are rights you can "exercise" after you've completed the initial rights run or executed the initial rights. You do not pay for these rights until you need them; however, most options need to be exercised within a 24-month period. What is beneficial about options is that you are given the up-front value, or cost, of those rights, which is helpful when negotiating your deal with a distributor. Most agreements give you up to two years to decide if you need those rights or not.

Here is an example:

- Initial rights: One-year film festival, worldwide—requesting $500/side.
  - Option: (a) all media rights in perpetuity—requesting $5,000/side;
  - Option: (b) digital media package including digital download and streaming rights for up to ten years;
  - Option: (c) DVD rights, advance on 5,000 units, U.S. only.

Many filmmakers tend to secure film festival rights as the initial rights and then secure a broad range of rights as an option. However, if the cost for those broad rights is too costly, it may be best to break those down even more. These days many films do not find distribution into theaters and are released directly onto a digital platform. This same group of films may also never see the light of day on television. So, in this case, a 'digital package' of rights would be more beneficial rather than 'broad rights.'

PRICE

The price of various rights is entirely subjective. Fees are generally based on a variety of factors:

The budget or nature of your film. Is the production an independent film under $1M or a Hollywood release? Is the production a non-profit with a 501c3 status or a promotional video by a corporate entity? The higher the budget, the higher the fee. Some licensors will ask what the 'music budget' is. Should you not have one, a good rule of thumb is to set aside 10% of your overall film budget toward music. This includes music licenses, supervision and composer work.

1. What media the production will be exhibited in. The greater the reach to audiences, the costlier the music will be. Streaming a production through the Internet provides a wider audience than showing the same production in a 300-seat theater. Exhibiting your film at a handful of select film festival screenings reaches fewer audiences than having it shown via a PBS broadcast.
2. What particular song, or band, is being used. Some songs are obvious 'hits,' which are going to be more costly than the same band's back-catalog material or a B-side song. For example, Aerosmith's "Back in the Saddle" will cost more than their more-obscure song "Chiquita." Independent artists who are not signed to major labels and major publishers also tend to be easier to obtain approval from, because they desire exposure and there is generally less administration and more direct contact with the artist. Many times artists themselves control their music and

can respond to a request quickly, eager to have their song placed. Major labels and publishers are contractually obligated to obtain permission from an artist or songwriter, usually through a representative such as a manager, who could be traveling, recording or simply unavailable. All these issues can delay turn-around time.

Some bands are simply unresponsive and do not agree to the use of their music in productions. At one time the band Arcade Fire did not license their music into any productions unless there was a relationship to Haiti. Prince was nearly impossible to license after his death due to estate issues. Frank Sinatra recordings were at one time priced prohibitively to the point where no one was using them. As time passed, interested parties would secure a Michael Bublé song instead, so guess what happened? You got it, now Sinatra masters are available to license, and somewhat reasonably. Since retail sales and streaming revenue are not what they used to be, synchronization licensing is one area they can't turn their backs on, unless they are really in a place to do so.

3. Those involved in the film. If a producer or colleague of the artist that you are requesting rights from endorses the project or is involved in the film in some way, a discount or favorable price can be garnered. This does *not*, however, mean that if the girlfriend of the roadie likes your project and says, "I know the band and they will give you the song for free," that the song is actually free. There must be actual proof, e.g., an email or letter, stating that the artist endorses the project—or, better, is a stakeholder in the project, in order to make the request more effective in your favor.

Copyright fees for synchronization licensing have changed dramatically over the last ten or fifteen years. Since media has changed, so have the licensors' desires to capture as much income as possible from synchronization placement. Film festival rights, which are generally obtained for one year, range from $500 to $1,000 per side, or $1,000 to $2,000 a song. This is rather low, because filmmakers are not compensated for the exhibition of their films in festivals and are seeking a distribution deal.

What they then should secure are some **option rights** prices per license for other media, so they know what to expect when their project locks in greater distribution. Here are some approximate fee ranges:

Media	Fee Range	Term
Theatrical	$1,500 to $3,000	Six months
Cable TV	$1,700 to $3,000	Five years
Streaming rights, no download	$1,500 to $3,000	Five years
Broad rights, step deal	$2,500 to $10,000	Perpetuity
DVD/digital download release: $0.15/unit, advance on 5,000 units – $750 perpetuity		

Corporate or advertising use of music, and music in games, tends to pay one flat fee for the intended use and the deals do not include options. Many times, should a company want to use a song for an intended production or product and they limit the term, for example to one year, a renewal of the same rights can generally be granted for the same fee with a 15% fee increase.

STEP DEALS

A step deal is when a filmmaker requires broad rights for distribution but wants to limit the financial exposure. This particularly pertains to documentary or independent films, since their success rate for recoupment of production costs may be low and their pocketbooks thin. Therefore they request an 'all media rights, step deal' in which they pay a fee up-front and then will pay again when their gross net receipts hit a certain threshold.

Here is a request example:

- Initial rights: one-year film festival, worldwide—requesting $500/side.
  - Option: all media in perpetuity, step deal starting at $2,500 with a step of $2,500 at $1M, $3M, $5M, and $7M.

Here are three examples of a step deal quote response:

A. Fee (based on 100% of composition): $2,500 initial fee, plus the following steps: + $3,000 due upon $1M, $3M, $5M, $7M and $10M worldwide gross box office receipts.
B. Terms: $3,000 initial fee MFN w/master and all songs. All media step deal (excluding in-context trailers, making ofs, featurettes and menu). Perpetuity. World.
   Additional payments of $4,000 due upon world gross revenue at steps of $500k and every $500k thereafter based on all forms of exploitation.
C. MEDIA: Broad Rights (Step Deal)—Initial Fee.
   TERM: Perpetuity.
   TERRITORY: World.
   FEE: $1,750.00.
   ADDITIONAL STEP FEES: Additional $1,750.00 step payments due @ $500K, $1M, $3M, and $5M world gross receipts based on all forms of exploitation.

Securing your rights in this manner allows for a payment up-front and then payments in the future once your gross receipts, which generally includes theatrical, television, videograms/DVD and all digital revenue combined. Clients who have reached this threshold, such as Lee Hirsh, director of the successful documentary Bully, say, "It's a good problem to have!"

MOST FAVORED NATIONS OR MFN

'Most favored nations,' often referred to as MFN, is a clause used while securing quotes. It means that if one licensor receives a certain fee, the others should be granted the same fee. Since many of the licensors do not communicate with one another, this is their way of inserting into the license or legal document that they must receive the same fee as either the other publishers of the song ('co-publishers in the production'), all music used in the project ('other publishers and masters in the production'), or songs of similar usage and/or timing ('all songs used in full'). The most common MFN quotes are those between publishers and masters—for example, for a one-year film festival license the publisher quotes "$500 (MFN with master)," and the master quotes "$1,000 (MFN with publisher)." When the uses are confirmed, the filmmaker would be obligated to pay $1,000 to the publisher and $1,000 to the label under the MFN provision of the licenses.

This clause can be a good one to have if you have a lot of songs in your production with the same value or stature. For example, we worked on a documentary about a photographer, with a soundtrack from the 1970s to reflect the era. The songs ranged from The Temptations' "Papa Was a Rollin' Stone" and Chic's "Le Freak" to Donna Summer's "Love to Love You Baby" and Marvin Gaye's "Got to Give It Up." All these very popular songs are controlled by only a few copyright holders and therefore all wanted the same fees as each other. No one was going to even think one song could garner more money than another!

The only time when MFN does not apply is if only one song in the production is of a much higher value—e.g., a Rolling Stones song—than all the others. One might think this is subjective; however, if that does become the case, it is possible to insert "MFN excluding the Rolling Stones song" in the license. That way the songs are on equal value, with the exception of the one song.

Lastly, in a film production, the song used over the opening and closing credits will be costlier, and therefore language can be inserted in a license to say "MFN with the exception of opening and closing credits." This would pull that song fee out of MFN and keep all other songs not used with the opening or closing credits at the established MFN rate. Here is an example by one licensor:

In consideration of the limited rights granted by this License, Licensee shall immediately pay Licensor the amount in Item 6 of Exhibit "A," to be paid without deductions of any kind or nature. Licensor's consent to the foregoing is given on a 'most favored nations' basis with all other sound recording and musical composition rights holders whose works are embodied in the

Program. To clarify the foregoing, in the event Licensee pays or agrees to pay to the publisher(s) of the compositions embodied within the Property a total fee greater than the License Fee paid to Licensor hereunder, Licensee shall promptly pay to Licensor the difference between such higher fee and the consideration paid to Licensor hereunder. Additionally, in the event Licensee pays or agrees to pay to the sound recording rights holder(s) of the masters embodied within the Property a total fee greater than the License Fee paid to Licensor hereunder, Licensee shall promptly pay to Licensor the difference between such higher fee and the consideration paid to Licensor hereunder.

Many filmmakers find the fees for licensed music to be out of their budget. Always remember you can secure step deals, which allow the user to lock in an initial right, e.g., Film Festival or DVD or streaming, which is paid up-front. Pre-negotiated options for any other media can be paid for if and when you need them. You can then opt-in within a reasonable time after the initial rights. This is a great way to manage costs for the life of your project, stretching out payments instead of paying larger fees up-front.

PUBLIC TELEVISION

The **Public Broadcasting Service**, or PBS, is an American television broadcaster that receives funding from the Corporation of Public Broadcasting (CPB), individuals and corporations. It is a not-for-profit entity that does not incorporate typical advertising, and a majority of the programming is sponsored by individual and corporate donors. For that reason, the CPB provides funding which covers the cost of the music licenses.

PBS was enacted in 1967 under the Public Broadcasting Act, which was signed by President Lyndon Johnson so as to be "carefully guarded from government or from party control." He stated, "It will be free and independent, and will belong to all of our people." Since then, federal money has been allocated to over 1,000 local radio (National Public Radio) and television stations (PBS) for programming and marketing purposes.

Any programs that are aired on PBS do not need to secure synchronization or master-use clearances for music broadcast on PBS, its affiliate stations and schools via satellite upload and streaming on their site, since the music licensing fees are covered under this funding. However, a cue sheet must be delivered so writers and publishers will be compensated under PBS's own statutory license. (Masters are exempt from fees for music heard on PBS under U.S. code Title 17, Section 114(b).) Yet please note that if your program secures distribution with a foreign television station, or is released on a different platform, such as DVD or VOD, the production company must secure music rights and pay for them in the standard manner since these rights are not covered under the CPB agreement.

Public broadcasting is a valuable part of America's educational outreach, providing both entertaining episodic productions such as *Downton Abbey*, *Sherlock* and *Victoria*, as well as renowned educational series like *NOVA*, *American Masters*, *POV* and *Independent Lens*. Let's hope that this outlet will remain supported by our government and generous individuals for a very long time.

7

BRAND PERSONALITY, IDENTITY AND RECOGNITION

People Rank Music as More Difficult to Live without than Sports, Movies and Newspapers

Consciously and unconsciously, consumers engage with countless brands every day. So many items we see are brands with a particular style, image or message. Individuals are inundated with images, both passive and overt, that are meant to remind us of the quality, innovation, beauty and reliability of products and experiences. We identify a trade name through an advertisement or banner in the media, and when music is used it can play a big part in this recognition. The combination of image and sound enhances any brand's message. It is therefore the task of the music supervisor or creative director to develop the sonic essence of the select brand. It is not an easy job, but when done successfully the result can impact products for a very long time.

There have been numerous studies that show how sound and music influence consumers to respond. Playing the right music in your boutique can make people stay longer. The right music played in a business that parallels the brand identity can positively affect one's opinion, so stores pump playlists to create atmosphere and aura around their products.

112 BRANDS

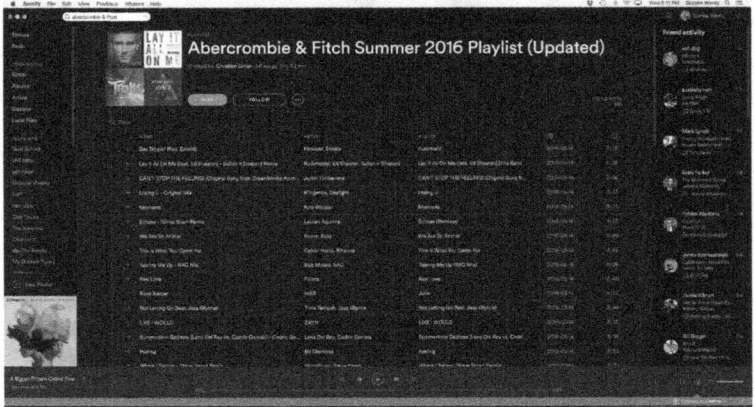

Figure 7.1 Spotify playlist

Renowned U.S. retailer Abercrombie & Fitch has such unique music played in its stores that it has a Spotify channel so customers can continue the experience away from the store or at home.

NPR writer Andrew Matson once said,

> A good retail playlist can bring home the culture of a business and psychologically affect a customer in a way that doesn't feel pushy. And it's positive for the featured artists. In today's flooded climate, where new songs are published at a crazy rate on the Internet, having your song play in a Victoria's Secret, for instance, can help cut through the noise....The amount of money changing hands is relatively small. But retail playlists are about making associations and building awareness. If your song is in every Gap in the world, it's going to get stuck in some heads. That's a connection. And that's what the store is trying to get in on.
>
> (November 28, 2012)

Studies have shown that certain parts of the brain react to sound and music in ways that have considerable impact. The 'Mozart effect' was a theory espousing that listening to classical music made toddlers smarter. Shortly after the information was published, children's products packaged with classical music flooded the market. Needless to say, the genre, tempo and volume of music played in a retail environment affects shoppers.

With an advertisement, which is short in length and has to communicate a brand's ideology or message within a very small window, music must be chosen well. Agency Goodby Silverstein & Partners' in-house music and creative producer Todd Porter had an experience when he found a song by a then-unknown band called Fun, with Janelle Monáe as a featured artist. The song was "We Are Young." Ingeniously, he and the creative directors talked the company's client Chevy into using the song in a Chevrolet Sonic campaign that premiered at the 2012 Super Bowl. Not only did the placement of the song help this band gain exposure to millions of viewers, but it also associated a Chevy with being youthful and free.

"The spot sent the song to #1 for six weeks," recounts a deservedly proud Porter, who received a note from General Motors' chairman saying how pleased he was with the music choice.

> It was one of the most successful ads Chevy has done. It was also a benchmark synch for us here at Goodby. The label, Warner Atlantic, loved how it came together, so everyone won. It was a well-timed placement for the band and would have never happened if it wasn't a good song; it was a great song.

Figure 7.2 OK Go

"Advertising creative directors communicate using color and feelings as references," explains former BBDO music director and music supervisor Chuck Bein. "There is a certain amount of guesswork involved when the supervisor is finding song selections for a client." The turn-around can be very fast and immediate. Many times, an in-house supervisor will need a song within a few hours and send an **ask** out to music licensing companies with the hopes of receiving songs by the end of the day.

Bein continues,

> Some agency creatives are good at what they want musically and so they record original music. But when those creatives don't know what to use, licensing a pre-recorded song is better. It's all about the people creating the spot's vision. I can send a creative director 25 tracks for consideration, and instead of them spending hundreds of hours having music composed they can choose from a selection of songs.

Although costlier than having original music composed for a spot, when a commercial song is chosen for an ad campaign and then licensed, the copyright can be secured on either an 'exclusive' or 'non-exclusive' basis. When exclusivity is placed on a song, generally no other brand or similar product type can use the same song for a chosen period of time within a select territory. This always increases the fee, and puts restrictions on the song's use. Non-exclusivity means no restrictions are included, and any other brand or like brand can use the song, although generally overlaps do not occur.

United Airlines built its entire brand campaign around the George Gershwin composition "Rhapsody in Blue." The company has re-recorded the song and made it its signature sound, using it in commercials, in-flight instructional videos and even as on-hold music. Few brands use a song to that extent. However, many music-centric campaigns have been very effective in drawing attention to a particular song, such as Feist's song "1234" for Apple's iPod Nano in 2007, or the Dirty Vegas song "Days Gone By" in a 2003 Mitsubishi ad, or the more recent use of Odetta's 1970s charmer "Hit or Miss" in the wonderful 2012 Southern Comfort ad. Even during the finale of *Mad Men* the producers cleverly unearthed the classic 1971 Coca-Cola **jingle** "I'd Like to Teach the World to Sing (In Perfect Harmony)." Viewers connected with its sentiment and it reminded all baby boomers of simpler times.

In the advertising world there are a variety of ways music is integrated. The most traditional is when a song or audio snippet, commonly known as a jingle or **mnemonic**, is composed specifically for a brand, like "I'd Like to Teach the World to Sing." Another option is to license a previously recorded, commercially available song, like "Hit or Miss," or re-record a popular song with a new twist or fresher feel. Some examples of this are Eminem's "Lose Yourself," which was covered by a gospel choir for the 2011 Super Bowl, or Israel Kamakawiwoʻole's cover of "Somewhere Over the Rainbow" for a Lynx/Axe ad, or José González's cover of The Knife's "Heartbeats" for Sony. Covering a song has become increasingly popular as it satisfies the viewers' knowledge of a known song with the intrigue of its new version and cuts down on licensing costs since it is not necessary to secure a master (previously recorded) license.

COMPOSING A JINGLE

Studies have suggested that music has become an important marketing tool in media productions, that today are consumed primarily on smart phones. Many people walk around with headsets, watching and listening to YouTube, Hulu, Vimeo, Tidal or Facebook. Pop-up ads are constantly preset before viewing desired content, and therefore the product's message must be succinct and immediate. Viewers' attention spans have shortened. What used to be a 30-second ad is now condensed to 5–15 seconds or less due to the Internet. Therefore, if music is going to be incorporated, the tone and mood must be immediate.

Chuck Bein explains,

> A jingle is when you are singing about the product. Lyrics are created to talk about the product. A mnemonic, or music designed to aid memory, can be as noteworthy because it is a bookend, a backdrop.

> There are definitely inefficiencies to having a jingle created. By not having a jingle created, the creatives don't have to make up their minds and define what they are looking for, which makes it easier for them. When you are having something composed you have to have a firm grip on exactly what it is you want, and you have to keep paying the composer until they nail it.

Composing music for a brand can work when a desired message is truly necessary. Jingles are songs written specifically for an advertising campaign to help promote a specific product. These songs are generally fun, upbeat and, most importantly, memorable. They tell stories about the product or exude an energy and feeling that parallels the experience of the product. Here are some classic examples:

- "Oh, I'd Love to Be an Oscar Meyer Weiner"—Oscar Mayer Weiner;
- "I'd Like to Buy the World a Coke"—Coca-Cola;
- "I Am Stuck on Band-Aid Brand 'Cause Band-Aid's Stuck On Me"—Band-Aid;
- "Every Kiss Begins with Kay"—Kay Jewelers;
- "Give Me a Break"—Kit Kat;
- "We Are Farmers"—Farmers Insurance.

This is not the most efficient way to work in today's rapidly changing industry, which is why we don't see too many jingles being created these days.

When brands commission artists to write and record original music for their campaigns, it leads to valuable income and exposure for the composer. Yet hiring the appropriate composer for this task is a unique experience. It is not like writing a pop song or ballad, so if you are involved in the hiring be careful who you choose. Many artists may want to try something new and feel they can write for commercials, but it is an entirely different skill set. Television and ad composers know that a good theme must be written in ten to fifteen notes. The best tactic is to cast a wide net and reel in select demos, and then choose among them and work with the company or individual who comes closest to your client's needs.

When hiring a composer for a campaign it is important to make very clear who owns the composition and master recordings. Many times, the corporate client will want to be in full ownership of the asset, or composition, that is being created for the campaign. The composer's copyright ownership must be clearly stated in the agreement right from the outset, as well as the use of union or non-union musicians. Generally non-union musicians will be involved, so no **reuse fees** will be incurred by the client and the music can freely be reused by it in different corporate or brand work. A reuse fee is an additional royalty fee paid to the musicians, singers or vocalists used on the recording session of the jingle. So when the jingle is reused for a purpose outside of the one for which it was recorded (e.g., a new commercial), the musicians are paid again as if they came into the studio and performed the music for that commercial. Having to pay reuse fees can be burdensome, which is why so many corporate clients would rather own the music they are commissioning outright than have to deal with third-party obligations later.

Another important aspect that the composer is responsible for is indemnifying the agency against any claims of sampling or plagiarism. The composer should never use others' music and claim it for their own, and so the hiring company must ensure that the music being created for the jingle does not make them liable for any possible infringement. The indemnity clause in the composer agreement should defend the producer against any lawsuits that may arise. To protect oneself, language such as this should be included:

- -

Composer hereby warrants, covenants and represents to Producer that it is the sole writer, creator and composer of the Score submitted to Producer hereunder, that the Score is original and does not (in whole or in part) infringe upon the copyrights, proprietary rights or any other rights of any third party or entity; that Composer has the full right, power and authority to enter into this Agreement and shall at all times have the full right, power and authority to transfer to Producer all rights to the Score, free and clear of any claim, lien or encumbrance by any third party; that Composer knows of no adverse claim or litigation by any third party; and that Composer has not made and will not make any use (or allow any use) of the Score which violates the terms of this Agreement or infringes upon Producer's exclusive rights to exploit the Score. Composer agrees to hold Producer (and its parent, subsidiary and/or affiliated companies) harmless from all liability for any breach or alleged breach of the representations and warranties herein and to fully indemnify Producer, its shareholders, officers, directors and employees and its parent subsidiary and/or affiliated companies, successors and licensees and assignees, from any and all losses, penalties, damages and/or expense, including attorney's fees, incurred as a result thereof.

- -

This language is good for any composer hired, whether it be for an ad or for a film. Plagiarism and copyright infringement are grounds for cease-and-desist letters that will make the hiring company stop airing or using the song immediately and pay a penalty for previous uses. The penalty fee will vary depending on how many uses the song has had in the particular production. A majority of the time, no copyright infringement cases get to court. Everyone always asks if they will get sued. No, you don't get sued. You typically get a cease-and-desist letter to avoid getting sued. Either way, neither eventuality is fun to deal with.

SONG PLACEMENT AND THE USE OF LICENSED MUSIC IN ADS

Many studies have shown that using previously recorded music in commercials is more effective than the use of words or slogans. Songs are better-remembered than scored music—excluding jingles—and are remembered even more when tied to a brand or image. Some examples include "Pink Moon" for Volkswagen, "1234" for Apple, and "Revolution" for Nike.

The hardest aspect of incorporating a commercial song in a campaign is acquiring permission for its use and negotiating a licensing fee. Any time a song is used in a commercial, the artist and songwriters must be contacted and the use must be approved by the appropriate parties. Denials are common when an artist does not like the brand, product, representation or offering fee, or they are already in an endorsement deal with a competing brand.

"The Black Keys license their songs quite a bit now," says Goodby's Todd Porter.

> But there was a time when they turned down every license. One time, I understand, one of the band members spoke to their parents about a potential placement that they were approached about and didn't want to do the ad. The parents chimed in and said, 'The money you will make from this one commercial is more money than what we paid for the house you grew up in. So you guys need to get your priorities straight!' The guys listened to their parents and accepted the campaign.

Chuck Bein recalls a story where he was involved in an Allstate commercial about drunk driving. He approached an artist about licensing a song, but they could not obtain clearance.

> We spent a week finding another song, and the second artist declined. It was 58 seconds of music and a multi-million-dollar deal, yet the artist said they didn't do commercials. Ultimately we got Skip Prokop from the band Lighthouse to write a piece. He took the subject matter to heart. One of his friends had died in a car crash in high school. He wrote a song over the weekend and when he came in with the demo and the creatives heard the song they started to cry. Skip nailed it over the weekend. He released a single, and the campaign was a hit.

Licensing a commercial song from the major labels and publishers has become increasingly expensive when exhibiting on new digital formats, i.e., streaming or video-on-demand. More companies are placing their advertising money into creating short streaming pieces and digital ads, so the licensors are now commanding higher prices for this platform of exhibition than television. In the past licensors included streaming in the rights when a company was also producing an ad for television. Today, since ad revenue has moved away from television and toward online placement, licensors recognize this and have increased their fees tremendously. What used to be $1,500 to $5,000 for the use of a song to stream online for a year is now up to $30,000 to $60,000.

"Internet use used to be a throw-away," explains Bein.

> Now the Internet has cost more since it is usually global by nature. There is also the time issue, with taking the spots down when finished. This pertains to talent obligations, especially when some companies who get hundreds of thousands of hits don't want to take down their spot. Therefore, Internet spots are also changing how they are acquiring talent.
>
> I'm seeing prices trending back up. Broadcast was $50,000 but now you can get five pieces created at $10,000. Custom work is rare for these fees and only bigger brands can afford custom for Internet streaming.

"I'm constantly on the phone with Sony/ATV and Universal," says Todd Porter.

> They have certain thresholds and it's difficult. Our clients are leaning more toward Internet and social media and the prices for streaming on the Internet and social media have totally changed since the beginning of 2016. I got a quote that was high, if not higher than, a television license would be. The quote was around $2 million for six months of Internet streaming…Something wild! That was for publishing only for Bruno Mars' and Mark Ronson's "Uptown Funk" for Super Bowl. To get a quote for legitimately Internet-only was shocking.

Granted, this fee was quoted at the height of the song's use, but when a song has multiple writers and publishers, such as "Uptown Funk," if one publisher quotes higher than the rest, the others will want to match it (as per the previously mentioned 'most favored nation' clause) and the higher quote can lose a deal for everyone involved.

Uptown Funk	Bruno Mars (ASCAP)	Mars Force Music c/o BMG Gold Songs (ASCAP)
	Jeffrey Bhasker (BMI)	BMG (ASCAP)
	Devon Christopher Gallaspy (BMI)	Way Above Music c/o Sony/ATV (BMI)
	Peter Gene Hernandez (ASCAP)	Thou Art the Hunger c/o WB (ASCAP)
	Philip Martin Lawrence (N/A)	WB Music Corp c/o Warner Chappell Music (ASCAP)
	Mark Ronson (BMI)	ZZR Music LLC c/o Universal Music (ASCAP)
	Lonnie Simmons (BMI)	Songs MP (BMI)
	Rudolph Taylor (BMI)	Songs of Imagem Music (BMI)
	Nicholas Joseph Williams (BMI)	Songs of Zelig c/o Imagem (BMI)
	Charles K Wilson (BMI)	Sony/ATV (BMI)
	Robert Lynn Wilson (BMI)	TIG7 c/o Songs (BMI)
	Ronnie James Wilson (BMI)	Trinlanta c/o Songs (BMI)

Film and television shows have more flexibility when licensing a song as they have more time to find another song should the fee be too high. Yet in the advertising world, there are so many creative and corporate approvals, or 'sign-offs,' companies would rather pay the higher fee to lock-in a song, since it is integral to the entire message of the ad.

A production company approached us about using the 1984 Prince song "Let's Go Crazy" for a **corporate** piece. A corporate piece is music a company uses at a trade show, streams online for its customers or employees or simply uses for a year-in-review-type piece to hold its head high.

These pieces are used generally not to advertise a single item but to promote or highlight events and products within a company. They are typically seen at large conferences or on the company's website only.

The request to use the Prince song came only three to four months after he passed, so it was a delicate negotiation to make. The description presented was:

The [client's] products are very much about creative joy, self-expression, experimentation and passion. The video spot will show a whole bunch of people—from artists to filmmakers to photographers to designers and beyond—making amazing stuff, with joy and passion.

This song is such a great expression of letting one's self go, putting critical voices (societies' or one's own) aside, and just expressing yourself however you want. No drugs, alcohol, sex, or violence is seen in the piece.

In addition, we love and adore Prince, and the use of the song is meant to signal that: he is missed by many, and we want to remember and celebrate him. In our current edit, we fade to black and let the guitar solo play out for an extended period. It's actually pretty moving.

As you can tell, the client was a huge fan, and the use was an overall feel-good piece. Through working with Prince's estate we were able to secure a one-day event exhibition and then, later, the ability to stream the piece on the client's site, only for a short period. This was not an easy task but one achieved through years of established connections, deep pockets, and approaching the estate at the right time. Not all requests like this come through but some are worth the push. This one was.

RE-RECORDING A KNOWN SONG

Another creative favorite becoming even more popular over the last few years is the **cover song**. This is when an artist, other than the one who made it a hit, re-records a known song. It's become a movie trailer trend recently (making a short 2–3 minute piece that previews an upcoming film) because listeners recognize the lyrics and music but hear a new voice associated with it. The new version adds a different twist to a known song, yet the new rendition also evokes a strong affinity to the original song. The best part about it is if the song is recorded for a specific project, the licensing will cost half the price because only the publishing rights need to be secured. When you re-record a song the original master does not need to be licensed, hence you only pay for the publishing.

"There are a number of reasons why re-records are in vogue now," says Todd Porter.

> The number-one reason is that it is a modern update of a classic song. It happens often. The idea is that you pull a song that everybody knows and you update it to a modern style or change the style and vibe to fit the brand message. That is the objective, but there are problems with this and good things about it.
>
> I spent three weeks covering a Carpenters song and found out that no one could do it better than the Carpenters. I covered it with a punk rock band to a hip-hop group, and it was painful. It's hard to reshape Karen's voice from the true meaning of the song.
>
> I have another project where we are covering classic 1980s and 1990s songs. The client is taking the Twisted Sister song "We're Not Going to Take It" and changing the lyrics to "You're Not Going to Watch It." I even got Dee Snider to perform at the end of the spot. It's a modern update and it's more of a parody, but it is a parody with actors singing it. This happens sometimes in campaigns.

Generally, the agency creatives brainstorm on songs whose lyrics are meaningful to their client. Initial quotes from the publishers are sought and then the music supervisor will find artists to cover the song. Sometimes, if a particular genre is desired a music house is called in to create an original cover. There are other times when the original will just have to do, and the agency may simply get actors to lip-synch the song in the commercial.

Figure 7.3 Carpenters—Close to You—1970

Music in advertising and trailers can potentially be one of the most effective and memorable uses of music with visual images. So whether or not you have a piece composed, license a commercial song or have a cover made, make sure the genre and lyrics align with the company's objective and style because the impact it can have on a product, and the users' perception of that product, is tremendous. Just look around you.

REFERENCES

Matson, A. (2012) "Who Picks the Music You Hear at the Mall?," NPR: The Record. November 28. Retrieved from: http://www.npr.org/sections/therecord/2012/11/28/165947927/who-picks-the-music-you-hear-at-the-mall.

8

DIGITAL MEDIA AND DIGITAL PLATFORMS

Welcome to the Digital Era in All Its Forms

The digital world moves so fast it seems that each year a new way to view media is announced. As of this publication, Snapchat went public—a company that literally offers its users the ability to share clips of tiny snippets of their life via smart phone. This then becomes user-generated video content, which means any copyrighted material would appear by happenstance; a girl 'snaps' her friends at a party and, lo and behold, music is heard playing in the background.

Over just the last ten years, it has been remarkable to see the different types of **digital platforms** that are available to exhibit a program. Content created today, whether a million-dollar production or a do-it-yourself video, will invariably stream online. This is no longer a trend; it's the norm. Today most viewers—millennials, mothers and grandmothers alike—are using their smart phones and tablets to access entertainment and news content from platforms like YouTube, Facebook, Instagram and Snapchat.

A digital platform refers to how content is being delivered, that is, how the viewer is accessing it. When you are watching content 'digitally' you tend to be accessing it over the Internet, streaming platforms or social media, or on your smart phone or video gaming console. So when it involves music rights, the concern is how the viewer is accessing the content that is defined as 'digital,' not the original format of the programming.

Understanding music licensing in the digital space is tremendously important. Digital is not actually a universally accepted term among rights holders. It's much more important to clearly define what one means by 'digital' when requesting music rights, so you are getting exactly what you need. If you are a student filmmaker, chances are your first production will be uploaded to a Vimeo page or YouTube channel or your school's official website. For this reason, a synchronization license would be required for the synchronized use of the music in your film in that exact media. We receive countless calls from people who think that because others have used music in a video on YouTube that it's fair game to use music in content uploaded on YouTube. It's not okay. Music uses, for the most part, over the Internet and over social media platforms require permission from the copyright holder.

Let's assume you are making a student film and you need to seek permission for a piece of music. The protocol is the same: engage the clearance process by sending a formal request to the music rights holders in the same manner as we've discussed before. You will undoubtedly be working off a very limited budget, so your media will be streaming on YouTube only, or on your university website for a very limited term, e.g., one year. This sounds easy enough. But assuming it's not an 'easy-to-clear' piece, like a popular song by the Red Hot Chili Peppers, the publisher(s) and label of the music will need to approve your limited use. At this point you only suspect you will be using Vimeo and your college website, and secure and license rights to only them. If, however, tomorrow you decide to place the video on a different social site such as Snapchat, your rights will need to be expanded. So unless you know exactly which sites—and by sites we mean the exact URLs on which the video will live—you plan to exhibit on, our recommendation would be to seek "Internet streaming rights" out of the gate.

Digital media definitions are confusing as the lines between different types of services and platforms get blurred. How services are defined and how to price each one is not so obvious. Some sites stream the media the minute you get to it, whereas on other sites the user has to trigger or press a Play button in order to get the media to start. Some sites have no built-in advertising whereas YouTube does, so the rights holders would want to know which sites you intend to stream your video on because the rights holders may be able to monetize on the back-end. Furthermore, YouTube acknowledges its position as a broadcaster, and as such it would be responsible for paying public performance income to the writers and publishers of the songs contained in the videos hosted on the site. Vimeo and Facebook, on the other hand, do not recognize themselves as public performance venues. As of the date of this book's publication, Vimeo's position remains that the onus is on the video uploader, not on the platform, to ensure proper clearance of the musical content contained in the videos they upload, including public performance rights. This is a space of contention for some publishers, such as Universal Music Publishing, which will specifically exclude Vimeo from an Internet streaming deal because it is either in negotiations about a deal concerning the treatment of its copyrights on the Vimeo platform, or Vimeo remains adamant that it is not a public performance venue and therefore should not be subject to the rules governing these types of sites. The point of this example is to show that today, ten years after the major influx in general entertainment user-generated video sites, we are still not at a place where the governance on these platforms is established. Things are still being worked out.

Whoever is to bear the burden of performance royalties, the prices for synchronization and Internet streaming rights are on the rise, whether requested by an indie filmmaker, a Netflix series producer or a major TV show. Viewers are "cord-cutting" and weaning off their cable subscriptions. They are beginning to view content over the web entirely instead of through television, and rights holders and advertisers are beginning to place equal if not greater value on streaming rights since more people are spending their time online. Take the example of the student filmmaker, who went the extra mile and secured a six-month streaming license for his film to show on his YouTube channel. The film earns great marks by students and peers alike, and wins a student competition led by his university. Now the university wants to upload the film to its website for archival use.

This is when things get complicated. His permission extended to YouTube only. Now he or the university will need to secure the additional rights to upload the film to another website, which will cost him or it. To avoid the back and forth, some secure all digital streaming rights up-front. Ordinarily this covers all platforms (websites, social media, etc.), but as we discuss later the cost is not cheap. And deals are often limited to one year, three years, or five years, because rights holders do not like the notion that their content can indefinitely live online. They want you to come back after a certain time so that they can re-up your deal and charge another license fee. This is why filmmakers are left piecemealing their rights packages: because, simply put, it saves them money today.

ALL INTERNET/DIGITAL STREAMING RIGHTS

Broad 'Internet/digital streaming rights' would be the best choice for almost any media producer intending to stream his content online. All bases would be covered, and a filmmaker would be able to freely stream or upload anywhere and anytime. Broad packages where digital rights are included also provide for download rights, which means the program could sell on Amazon or iTunes. Here are the rights covered under this package, and popularly used definitions of them:

- **'Internet Streaming'** shall mean the transmission at a time of the user's choosing by Internet or other computer network protocol (as applicable) of a constant flow of data to the end user for the immediate exhibition of the Program.
- **'Internet Downloads'** shall mean the distribution by Internet or other computer network protocol (as applicable) of the Program in electronic format whether time limited, play limited, permanent, or otherwise regardless of means of data retention.
- **'Wireless/Mobile'** shall mean the exhibition of the Program via transmission by radio waves or other wireless communication methods to mobile (i.e., portable) viewing devices, including, but not limited to, cellular telephones and tablet computers.

- **'Free on Demand (FOD)'** shall mean the exhibition of the Program via a television-based service at the time of viewers' choosing whereby viewers are not charged a separate fee for such capability.
- **'Video-on-Demand (VOD)'**: 'Paid VOD' and 'Bundled VOD' shall mean the exhibition of the Program for which viewers select specific programs to be transmitted to them via Cable TV at a time of their choosing either (i) for a fee per selection ('Paid VOD'); or (ii) bundled as part of a Basic Cable TV or Pay Cable and Subscription TV service fee (i.e., transmission without a fee per selection) ('Bundled VOD').

Depending on the term sought for an all-digital package (e.g., three years, ten years, perpetuity), we have seen fees range from $1,500 to $7,500 per side. This is fairly common and is largely attributable to the budget and nature of the film (independent documentarian vs. motion picture studio), and, of course, the caliber of the artist or song. But even $1,500 per side for one song is a steep price to pay for an independent filmmaker. Especially when it's not certain whether or not you will need broad rights. If you can afford them, lock them in. You never know what lies ahead, especially in digital media. For the documentary *Big Voice*, filmmaker Varda Bar-Kar made a push for pre-sales on iTunes as part of her film's distribution plan. This was essentially digital download and streaming on iTunes. Once a certain threshold of buyers pre-bought the film to stream or download on the platform, *Big Voice* was granted greater visibility on the site. The greater visibility led to even more pre-sales, and this popularity brought her attention and gave her leverage in making the film's Netflix deal. Luckily for the filmmaker, broad digital rights had been secured, so when the Netflix deal came to fruition Bar-Kar could freely enter into it without concern for music rights. Had broad digital rights not been secured, she would have had to go back to the rights holders to renegotiate for Internet streaming rights. Ultimately that would have cost her more money.

It is essential for filmmakers to drill down to exactly what they need so they are not left having to come back and request additional platforms later. Since there are a multitude of ways audio-visual productions can be exhibited online, and a variety of rights you will need for each, it is an ever-changing landscape and it is important to understand it.

VIDEO-ON-DEMAND STREAMING SERVICES

Perhaps the most popular viewing preference is VOD. It allows the user to watch films and television shows when they want—on-demand—rather than at a specific broadcast time. Conventional VOD is cable-based—an extension of your cable subscription making certain programming available when you want it through your cable box. Bravo, CNN, MTV and hundreds of other networks and channels offer their subscribers the opportunity to catch favorite shows after initial broadcast. The box also provides exclusive content such as pay-per-view and special events like the Olympics or World Cup. Even conventional VOD has online offerings. HBOGo, for example, gives the cable subscriber the ability to access HBO content on their mobile, tablet or Apple TV.

By contrast, Internet-based VOD services stand on their own two legs. They offer traditional network television shows, movies and other general entertainment video content online, either from the content owner directly or from third-party services, and users can access the content on any number of compatible devices. Examples include Netflix, Hulu, Amazon, Google, Vimeo and YouTube. Depending on the VOD service or platform, the programming is made available for free (peer-to-peer or user-generated), for rent or purchase/download (iTunes, Amazon Instant Video, Google Play), or under a subscription-based model (Netflix, Amazon, Hulu). There is also in-flight VOD and even special-market VOD that you see at gas station pumps. There are so many different ways to access audio-visual content, and the list continues to grow as technology affords viewers more and more possibilities.

In the independent feature and documentary world, specifically, more and more films are being picked up at festivals and go straight to digital distribution. This is a good thing because delivery requirements for most buyers, or distributors, will then only involve 'digital media' rights from the filmmaker, which is one-third to one-half the cost of an 'all media' rights package, and fees will be considerably less. If the filmmaker is lucky enough to be called upon to secure 'all digital' rights (many distribution deals for streaming companies like Netflix and Hulu still expect you to secure all-media rights), fees will be considerably less. Yet even these prices are steep. Publishers and labels are savvy and know more traditional television viewers are moving online so VOD and digital rights deals are becoming increasingly more expensive. We recommend sending your distribution deal language to your music supervisor so proper rights can be secured. If a deal is in negotiations, they can also serve as advocate to a filmmaker during this time. Services like Netflix request filmmakers secure all media rights, despite being a streaming only platform. A music supervisor can step in and help modify the deal terms by pursuing Netflix only rights or VOD only rights, serving both the platforms requirements while respecting the filmmakers tight budget.

OPTIONS

"When you are involved in a price-conscious production, options are a great approach," says a senior director at a leading publishing company. Options give a licensee the right, but not the obligation, to exercise permission to exhibit their film in another media for a pre-negotiated price under the contract. Options are beneficial because they allow for up to 12 to 24 months to exercise and pay for the rights if and when you need them. It's like getting a quote for something, and locking it in, without having to pay for it until you need to.

The publishing director continues by saying,

> Traditionally, television deals would cover two sorts of television rights—free TV, i.e., broadcast television networks, ABC, NBC, CBS and Fox—and basic cable: MTV, USA, Disney, CNN. The music licensors will price each out separately and then provide an option fee for pay-per-view, and an option fee for broad VOD. This way the production can pick and choose the rights they want to exercise. But remember, if you exercise all of them, you would pay more than if they secured all-media rights up-front.

True, but if you don't have all the money to pay for these rights up-front, options can help alleviate cash flow issues.

This is why it is important to assess what term and media rights are absolutely necessary for a production. Be realistic, because going back for additional rights is never cost-effective. For example, you may need one streaming service today and maybe a different one tomorrow. How do publishers price these? "I look at one service against another service," says the publishing executive.

> It could be the same program and similar concept. So if I charge the client $3,000 for Netflix, maybe I charge them another $1,500 for Amazon. I think when clients are budget-conscious, and they know they will want multiple platforms, I recommend they secure all the rights even if they will be paying a little more.

We have seen this scenario play out many times.

STEP DEALS

As mentioned in Chapter 6, negotiating a **step deal** is another way to curb costs. These deals allow for a conservative up-front fee, and then monetary bumps, or 'steps,' at different milestones. Traditionally, these are offered under all-media rights deals where the initial fee is, for example, $1,000. If and when certain box office sales milestones are reached ($1M, $3M, $5M), the production would pay additional 'bump' (or payment) of $1,000 at each million-dollar milestone. We are seeing variations of this in the digital space. Instead of box office steps, the bumps are instead triggered when 'gross receipts on all forms of digital exploitation'—from streaming or downloads—are reached; for example, at $250,000, $500,000, $750,000 and $1,000,000. As we previously discussed, the idea is that as the film earns money, so do the copyright holders. However, this approach has not been adopted by all. "I question whether or not those companies are triggering their steps," says the publishing company licensing director. "Are they self-reporting? 'Oh, I owe you more money, here it is.' I'm doubtful that's happening." Today there is no way to monitor streams or plays. The licensing director adds, "I think there are ways that it could be policed, but is it worth the cost of policing?" *Variety* does so on box office receipts. *Variety* is a reputable trade magazine that publishes the gross box office earnings of films, so it serves as a source of trusted information when assessing whether or not a film has reached its 'million milestones.' The only way to assess streaming or plays is by asking for this information from the specific streaming service, and of course reliability is called into question.

YOUTUBE

The question comes up constantly. Do you need a license for YouTube? The answer is, absolutely. Yet with 1 billion videos posted on YouTube, does one assume that every single video has had their music rights cleared? What about the guy who posted the video of his flash-mob marriage proposal to the music of Bruno Mars? Or the hundreds of videos people uploaded of them singing "Happy" by Pharrell Williams? Did they really seek permission from every rights holder? The answer is no. 'User-generated content' on YouTube is handled differently. YouTube will generally take care of the licenses required to stream so-called non-commercial or user-generated content. These are based on previously negotiated deals YouTube has made with the rights holders. Each rights holder simply monetizes the videos and earns ad revenue. There is no negotiation or license fee up-front.

But remember, this only covers user-generated content. If your video has any commercial value, like a film or an advertisement of goods or services, then this pre-negotiated license does not extend to your use, and you will need to seek permission.

YouTube uses a content management system. This dashboard tracks the ownership of all the assets (video, music and sound recording) supplied to it by content owners. The second you upload a video to the system, it is scanned for third-party content and you will be informed if there are any copyright claimants.

If you receive a notification from YouTube, all you need to do is acknowledge the third-party's ownership and not claim the audio on the

> Your video may include a song owned by a third party. For example, this might be a song playing in the background or someone performing a song.
> To hear the matched song please play the video on the right. The video will play from the point where the matched content was identified.
>
> Your video is available and playable.
> If this video is your cover of a song written by somebody else, you may be eligible to monetize this video.

Figure 8.1 YouTube copyright notification message

exhibiting YouTube channel. This basically signals to them that the rights holder, not the video producer, is able to monetize the video. Rights holders may also decide to block a video containing their assets. This happened recently with one of our action sports producers. We cleared a Ludovico Einaudi track for an online ad that was going to be streamed on YouTube. Both the publishing and the master rights were cleared and licenses entered. Yet YouTube sent this notice:

The notice came as a surprise to them since we had cleared and entered licenses for the use of the music. In this case the block was the result of a previous copyright claimant. Things can get sticky when copyrights switch hands regularly. The blocker in this case owned distribution rights to the music, but not the synchronization rights. The client was entirely lawful in his use, but the distribution company's notice appeared and the client was stuck in a jam. Today most publishers and labels advise clients on how to handle a blocked video. If you receive one of these messages *do not challenge* the claim as that may result in a strike to your YouTube account. Instead, contact the publisher or label (or your music supervisor), give them the URL containing the blocked video, and they will contact the licensor to have the claim lifted. For this reason, we often advise our clients to upload their videos prior to official release dates. This will afford you the time to remedy any unforeseeable copyright issues arising from the upload. Also, the system simply identifies copyrights. It does not know what synchronization licenses are being negotiated or have been entered into by the producers and licensors. For this reason, we advise that once a deal is struck, 'test upload' your video so that you can troubleshoot issues early.

Another aspect that many users feel allows them to post at-will on YouTube is the 'fair use' claim. Knowing what is 'fair use' exactly is hard for a user to assess, since these sorts of claims are what a lawyer can best attest to. Therefore, YouTube has a page that describes fair use and states the following about this issue:

> YouTube receives lots of takedown requests under copyright law asking us to remove videos that copyright owners say are infringing. Sometimes those requests target videos that seem like clear examples of fair use. Courts have held that rights holders must consider fair use before they send a copyright takedown notice, so in many cases (though it's a very small percentage of copyright takedowns overall), we ask rights holders to confirm they've done this analysis.

Please refer to our previous description about fair use as this is a complex matter about which many books have been written.

SOCIAL MEDIA

Social media sites like Facebook and Instagram are also popular platforms for video sharing. They operate much the same way as YouTube, in that licensors will want to know which platform(s) your video will be on, so as to determine whether or not revenue is being generated or if ad money is being spent, or whether it will be on a platform that holds a public performance license. If either of those situations is taking place, the licensor feels they should be paid appropriately as well. Therefore, it is important to specify which social platforms will stream the video and whether there will be paid boosts.

DIGITAL MARKETING AND ADVERTISING

As we have discussed, online video has quickly become the key means for people to satisfy their information and entertainment needs, and advertisers know it. According to a recent Nielsen poll, approximately 65% of advertisers believe more money will be spent on brand marketing online this year. This increase in online marketing budgets is being recognized by all, including the publishers and labels.

When seeking the rights to use music in a digital ad, the length of the spot and the number of spots become very important. Time and time again we see clearances for a 90-second 'long-form' ad spot. We clear the rights for YouTube and social media streaming for one year for an indie film trailer, and the fee comes back at around $5,000/side. Then the client tells us that there will be a 'short-form' edit as well, and a 60-, 30-, and 15-second **pre-roll** edit. Yikes! A pre-roll piece is an online video advertisement that plays before the start of a video that has been selected for viewing. This is not good, because although it seems this would be a small nuance, it has major consequences—particularly regarding the fee. These are actually four unique videos, not one. Even when based on the same creative concept, rights holders want to know and have control over the dissemination of their content, and this requires transparency at the start of negotiations. Simply because these are short versions of the same ad, they all need to be cleared and communicated to the rights holder. Most importantly, because the additional edits involve additional money, so the fee that was $5,000/side is now $7,500/side.

This approach is also subjective and the additional fees are entirely the call of the licensor. A client licensed the Gloria Gaynor hit "I Will Survive" for an online-only teaser for a game, and although the ad spot totaled 60 seconds, the cut down to a 30-second spot was included in the fee. No change to the creative work was made; a shorter version of the same piece was simply made available for ad placement.

Additionally, when ad agencies or branding companies seek permission to use a song as part of an online campaign, the request for rights must be very specific as to whether or not the synchronization use will be visible on the Internet for all to see, or on a secure, employees-only site called **Intranet**. This distinction makes a huge difference regarding price. The fee for Internet use could range from $10,000 to $80,000, whereas use on an Intranet might be between $3,000 and $10,000 depending on the song and client. What we are trying to impress here is to be prepared to answer a variety of questions concerning the video. Even where there is doubt as to whether or not the video is an innocent lifestyle piece with little to no branding or whether it's a full-blown advertisement, err on the side of advertisement (because that is how the rights holders see it). Have your answers ready. On what platforms will the video live and for how long? What is the length of the video and will there be pre-roll and/or cutdown versions? Is there any paid media and if so what is the length of the media buy? Will there be cross-promotion with other brands? Come to the table with your ducks in a row, because the rights holders surely will.

VIDEOGAMES AND APPS

"For digital, broadly speaking, games is a huge market," says our colleague at a leading publishing house. "Fifteen years ago, video game rights just weren't there. It wasn't until *Guitar Hero* that games started to receive attention."

Console gaming, social gaming or virtual reality, composed score or original music—if you are using licensed music the process is the same. Generally, however, licenses are granted for a flat fee and are restricted by the term. A game that wishes to use a piece of music in perpetuity, or forever, will pay more for the license than it would for a term of ten years, for example. The flat fee generally makes it easier to license, due to the re-play action of the user. A film may be watched only a handful of times, whereas a game may be played over and over again.

Apps are no different. An industry that truly stepped into being a mere few years ago is a dominating force in the digital licensing space. Our office receives many calls from app developers. They are building an application that will use music in some form or another—a song lyric guessing game, a version of Hangman which uses song lyrics, tablature or chord reproduction apps, apps that allow users to generate video content from copyrighted material . . . You name it, we've heard about it. Here's where it gets tricky. If the game reproduces the lyrics, simultaneously streams the audio for the music, and, on top of that, allows users to generate their own content and share it among their friends, this developer should be ready to pay a minimum of $50,000 to each major music publisher and label to get his business off the ground. In most cases, the rights holders would become partners and share in the revenue of the business, given that their content makes up the game or app. Deals like this are high-volume and require blank 'digital gaming' licenses.

Alas, *Digital* can mean a lot of different things when it comes to content delivery. Each service and platform may offer different things, so when requesting music rights be clear and specific. Streaming on YouTube as a pre-roll online video advertisement is different from streaming rights on your official website. It's the same for Facebook. Be safe, not sorry. If you know you will sign a Hulu deal and you just might want to shop the film around to other platforms, secure all digital rights out of the gate. In the long run it will be less costly.

9

FOR THE ARTIST

There Is a Musician in All of Us

The placement of music into TV and film, and now video online, has become a rapidly growing area of income for musicians and writers, all clamoring for the opportunity to have their music heard by music supervisors. Although this book was written for media producers, we've put together some thoughts for artists about presenting their material to media creators.

One of the best avenues for an artist to get synchronization placement is to know music supervisors. As previously discussed, these are independent music experts who assist media producers with sourcing the right music for their project. A knowledgeable supervisor will have numerous sources to choose from to service their clients. An artist should know what the supervisor's specialty is and what projects they are working on. For example, you would not pitch a supervisor working on a period show such as *Narcos*, which takes place in Colombia during the 1980s, techno or contemporary music. Likewise, you would not generally pitch a popular network sitcom period music like jazz or R&B, unless the show specifically called for it.

Beautifully overdone, there is an excerpt from the HBO series *Girls* (Season 5, Episode 7) where they farcically re-enact the importance musicians put on music supervisors. The character Desi races in to tell Marnie about a song of theirs that has been placed in *Gray's Anatomy*. Yes, artists do believe a music supervisor can jump-start their career through the placement of a song on a show. Renowned music supervisor Randall Poster says, "Movies, media, commercials are kind of like radio in a way, so definitely a good placement is going to give a band or an artist a profile that they wouldn't otherwise have." Yet it is the circumstance of the job, not a function of it, and therefore artists need to keep churning out great music and maintain relevancy after the placement to achieve true success.

As an artist you may have colleagues who are filmmakers or music supervisors, and so the ability to give your material to them might be simple, whereas other artists have no clue how to get their music in front of supervisors or producers, and how, as a media creator, can you receive music or stay aware of artists who are keen to use their music?

There are music catalog representatives who can help musicians get their music heard, and there are various digital platforms that a filmmaker or media producer can use to stay abreast of new music. Those representing catalog and artists are called catalog reps or **song reps**. They have vast lists of contacts and the ability to know what shows, productions and supervisors need on an ongoing basis. A lot of these companies, or individuals, are based in Los Angeles, New York, London and Paris, close to where many productions are happening. Yet new businesses have opened in Seattle, Austin, San Francisco and Montreal. Catalog reps pitch the catalog for placement opportunities, usually earning a commission based on a percentage of the license fee in addition to or in place of a salary.

Andre Comeau, a recording artist and original cast member of the very first reality TV show, MTV's *Real World New York*, and now a senior creative services director at a leading licensing company, says about working with music supervisors and trailer houses, "People are generally pretty friendly and want to hear good music. But it is a dance . . . If you are not abrasive and annoying you can get their attention."

"All the music supervisors want to hear new music and help discover what the great new thing will be," he continues. The supervisors love discovering and introducing new music to directors. "They can be that key person in the link that makes it happen. But if a catalog rep pushes too hard, or does not do the dance right, they can be blacklisted and won't be taken seriously."

If you are a contracted artist or songwriter for a major label or publisher, it is the job of your record label or publisher to help exploit your catalog and get your songs in front of the right music supervisors and directors. They do this so you, as the artist, can focus on your craft and produce more songs. Essentially the media producer is the buyer, and the artist, individual or rep is the seller. These sellers have only a select group of content that they harvest from their catalog. So if they don't have what the buyer needs, the buyer moves elsewhere.

Most sellers pitch to in-house music directors of television networks, film studios, music supervisors, trailer houses and creative directors at ad and branding agencies. So, for the most part, these in-house folks will be bombarded with music options. The hardest part for the buyer is to suss out all their options and narrow them down to those sources they like to use, and who is the most pleasurable and easy to work with. Many companies have a distinct sound, or represent a particular music genre. Others may have a deep catalog, like Sony Music or Universal, and the reps will be more interested in knowing what your project is about so they can narrow their offering to you.

When an artist submits music it is very important that all the information is labeled properly. This labeling with all pertinent information is called the **metadata**. This data includes the writer(s) name(s), publishing company/companies and the percentage of ownership splits of the writers (e.g., Joe Blow controls 60% and Jim Jones controls 40%), designating who owns what percentage of a song.

Music supervisor and coordinator Ben Sokoler at Metalman Media says, "The biggest issue we have is artists not labeling folders of music and so we have no idea who it came from."

A prepared artist rep will have all the metadata tools and MP3s ready before pitching material to a media producer. Andre Comeau explains,

> If an artist wants to succeed in music licensing, they must go the extra mile to make sure that everything they do is handled in the most efficient and professional manner. That includes every element of metadata that you can think of—company name, contact, ownership, email, phone number, splits, the performing rights organization and percentages.

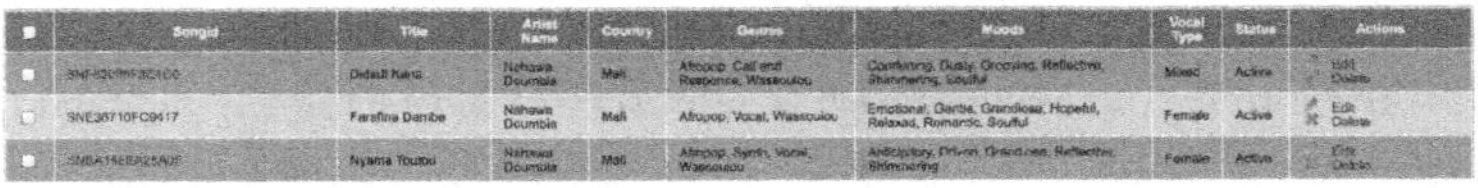

Figure 9.1 Metadata management tool

A great tagging tool available to almost everyone is iTunes. Any uploaded file can be custom-tagged in the 'Get Info' section. This metadata lives in the digital file, so when it is downloaded the details go with it.

According to many catalog representatives, a WAV file should never be sent, nor an MP3 within an email, unless the filmmaker has specifically requested it as such. WAV files do not carry metadata. These larger files are generally requested once a song is placed in a project, so it is best to send MP3s in a downloadable link.

It is also never good to send a prospective client to a YouTube link. On YouTube you can preview a song but not necessarily download it. Although artists want to protect the ability to not have their music shared around the world, when sending music to a potential buyer they need the actual file. Media producers can do nothing with a YouTube or SoundCloud link, unless the SoundCloud stream allows for download. Understand that if you are keen for others to listen and use your music in a production, music supervisors are not the enemy and need to be able to access it, download it and have the contact information in one click.

Artists starting to explore this area of revenue should also manage their expectations. Ben Sokoler advises, "Don't expect ten synch placements within the first month. Start off by sending a twenty-song sampler with no more than 100 megabytes. Always include your contact information and licensing contact."

He adds, "A lot of artists have a hard time putting their music to certain programs." He tells one story about a Christian band who wanted to change their image and go more mainstream, so they decided to no longer license their material for Christian programs. "Artists can be picky sometimes. If they want to get their music into select shows, they have to be open to opportunities."

Filmmakers and advertising agencies generally have a longer period for auditioning their music due to the long creative process, the importance of the track and the licensing fee. Television and trailer uses tend to have a quicker turn-around time, but in general music often needs to be found within a 24-hour period, which makes it even more important that metadata be accurate.

Many times a request or 'ask' to catalog reps is sent for a specific piece of music, and the music needs to be delivered by the end of the day or within 24 hours. This is particularly true with ad agencies, television and trailer houses. Filmmakers have more lead time. Here are some examples of music request briefs:

Trailer Spec

Hi everyone: We're starting on a new super-cool project and we're looking for songs with lyrics about A NEW WORLD, A NEW FRONTIER, REVOLUTION, A NEW UNIVERSE, SEEING IN A NEW WAY, EMERSION, CHANGING PERCEPTION, DAWN OF A NEW AGE, SUNRISE ON A NEW DAY, CROSSING TO THE OTHER SIDE, BREAKING THROUGH . . . Could be a big hit tune from any time period—open to Great American Songbook, musicals, classic rock, soul, jazz standards, pop, rock, indie rock, alternative rock, current jams . . . Open to originals as well as cool cover songs and remixes, and to big instantly recognizable songs or a really, really cool unknown or smaller artist . . .

Deadline is tomorrow at 1pm—thank you so very much for your attention and in advance for your hard work!

Commercial Request

Hi all: Song about the potential for something better in your life. It's about striving for more or stepping up to a higher level. Lyrics like The Beatles'

"Getting Better" would work great. The typical sound is upbeat, indie pop. Can be electronic or any other genre that has a good time, fun, positive feel. They are open to re-recording if the lyrics are great and the vibe isn't quite right.

Film Request

Looking for high-energy indie rock with electronic instrumentation tracks that have drive and lyrics about 'we're the first,' 'we're the best,' 'we're on the cutting edge,' 'we will win,' 'it's new, new, new!' 'change your thinking,' etc. Lyrics should be impactful. Tracks need to be upbeat, confident and catchy. Edgy pop appeal is important, with a hook that will get stuck in the listener's head. Thanks!

Almost every month, creative directors at labels and publishers generally send out new releases to music directors and supervisors, as well as in-house film and television departments and trailer and ad houses. CDs used to be the general mode of delivery, but these days download links are sent. The reps follow up in hopes of landing a placement. Fees for placements can vary depending on the nature of the project. With a 'call out' there are generally many songs thrown into the pot so it is the luck of the draw to win the coveted placement.

If artists have independently released their own recording, or if the label is small enough that they don't have the in-house manpower to land synchronization deals, they sometimes hire an agent or placement company. These are independently run businesses that work full-time to place music. They look to film, television, ads, trailers and corporate work. Many also handle publishing administration and become more involved in managing catalogs.

These reps act as brokers and generally take a portion of the synchronization fee. However, there is a some contention around those select few placement companies that also do what is called **re-titling**. Not as common as previous years, but something to be aware of, re-titling is when the representative places a song in a production, and they re-name the song in order to claim a portion of the publishing. This allows the rep to receive back-end income, or royalties, from the public performance of the song he or she placed. This can be substantial if a song lands in a production aired on television. This alternative title is given to the song so the composer does not need to transfer the original copyright. The writer maintains their 100% share and the re-titler takes anywhere from 50–100% of the publishing of the re-titled song. With more content being seen on streaming platforms where very little performance income is generated, or is insignificant to claim, re-titling is used less frequently.

It is hard these days, with so much music available, to get heard above the noise, but it is possible. If your music has the right lyrics or the right feel for a particular series, and the supervisor or director has it on hand, with all the proper information, this can be golden. Contact information, which includes an email address and phone number—yes, phone number—is very, very important for artists if they are interested in synchronization use of their music. We cannot tell you how many times no contact information is available. When there is nothing to go by, we find their Twitter handle and tweet them, or search on Facebook for a contact. Generally, however, if the contact info is not quickly available, and no one gets back within the day, the opportunity is commonly lost.

On the other hand, we've seen artists respond immediately and a deal can be done in 20 minutes. This happened with the Czech alternative rock band DVA: they responded to a tweet and we were able to lock down a deal within a few days. The client and artist were both thrilled.

Much like getting a job, timing also has a lot to do with music placement. If a supervisor is working on a film taking place in Mississippi and the right acoustic banjo music comes across their desk that week, it will probably be given more attention than the angst-ridden love song about break-ups. There is no rhyme or reason, or guarantee. Many times a song will fit a scene and then the scene is cut at the last moment, or the director has decided to go in a different direction. Whatever the situation, you have ebbs and flows. Some careers of artists have changed dramatically from the right placement, and others haven't seen a dime. Yet seeing a credit at the end of a show can bring a smile and, better yet, a nice clip to have in your back pocket.

10

CONCLUSION

Parting Words of Encouragement

Music is an awesome addition to any project! Everyone loves musicians and their hard-earned efforts, their poetic lyrics, their driving rhythms and the solace and joy songs bring to life. The rights clearance aspect is simply one hurdle that has to be tackled when wanting to use music in media.

Music rights themselves have not become more complex; only the system surrounding them has. There are more media to consider and each has different delivery requirements for producers. We all know the protocol is onerous, sometimes costly and time-consuming, but in the end creatives are being enumerated for their efforts. With dwindling income to artists through CD and digital download sales, they look to filmmakers, producers, directors and gaming companies to hire them and license their music. This way they make a chunk of money, and potential royalties, without doing much (additional) work.

Consumers have given the recording industry flack over the way it has handled copyright infringement cases, and music conglomerates have been chided about not adapting to change as fast as their digital-media constituents. Yet labels are historically creatures of habit. They are aware of the changing landscape in music licensing and realize it does call for a faster solution to parallel the digital change. Unfortunately, their old contracts and protocol have not allowed them to move fast enough. Let's all make money, folks!

Media is being created at a greater speed now than ever before. There are more television and cable networks. There are many digital streaming platforms and there is YouTube. Even streaming content distributors are creating original content—Netflix, Amazon, The Orchard, Refinery29 and more. There are mobile apps. There are moving billboards, mobile content, in-flight options. There are even art pieces with embedded content. Most of today's media is being created to marry music with images. As the system would have it, the copyright holders must grant permission before the media creators can use the music. Yet, ironically, those copyright holders cannot speak for their clients. Most publishers and record labels must contact the songwriters and artists, in some cases their estates, to seek approval, which can take weeks or even months. Writers are too busy trying to connect with one another to give their consent to a request. Even if an artist is quick, there are often internal approvals within the labels themselves that seem to slow the process. One client came to us simply to follow up on a clearance of the Jack White song "Hello Operator." They requested the song in June and hadn't heard anything from his label until, in late September, the label wrote, "Hey, still working on this for you. Will get you an update ASAP." Thankfully, we got approval by November.

Film and TV personnel must check if there are any conflicts. Is the song you wish to use under an exclusive license for a different or competing client? Is the use consistent with marketing efforts for that artist's album? Further, is the proposed license fee even worth their time? Some artists can't be bothered. If, through no fault of the artist, one is left with the message that a particular artist is difficult to clear, the music supervisor may not go back to them again.

When a pile of requests stack up at the label's office that need processing, and your film-festival license is competing with a nationwide ad campaign, which do you think the label will address first? The one offering the most money. Licensing teams at these companies are understaffed and overworked. Good people at the labels and publishing companies are often lost. This results in replacement staff that may not have those long-term relationships with supervisors, but many companies are really attempting to turn around requests faster. Sometimes the requests that get the attention are the ones from those with the loudest bark. The process does take time but is worth the effort.

Labels and publishers who own and control the rights of the music should be able to speak on their clients' behalf, but many cannot. They must go to the anonymous approving party and wait for a reply. This slows the process and a common response is, "I'm still waiting on my approval party."

Some labels are seeking new ways to make revenue for their artists. They are funding music documentaries to generate interest in their catalogs (*Amy* was initiated by her label Universal Music Group), acquiring production companies (Eagle Rock was purchased by Universal Music Group) and even partnering with artists who have done a great job building their brand over various platforms and audiences (Justin Bieber). With this cross-industry growth, companies are seeing weakened productivity because their core business has been diluted. They are trying to be a jack of all trades. Some have done it well, like Disney, dominating in radio, amusement parks, television, publishing and recordings. Others have not been so successful.

Recognizing this flawed system has allowed for a new breed of music licensors. Labels have noticed the ease and quick turnover of one-stops and have jumped on board and are acquiring them. Even the publisher Warner Chappell and its label side, Warner Entertainment Group, are working together to streamline licensing, giving licensees the opportunity to work with them under a single umbrella.

If popular music is what you want, then be ready to jump in head first and negotiate. Remember, prices are subjective, so you can negotiate with the copyright holder to a point where you are both comfortable. Be realistic and anticipate challenges. Know that you will need time and patience to curate the perfect soundtrack. For documentaries, involve a lawyer early in the process to assess your project for fair-use material, avoiding the need to license an expensive song you thought would be so difficult. Remember to involve a composer sooner rather than later in a project, and when seeking to a use a hit song be prepared for high fees and a difficult negotiation, or a straight-up lack of negotiation. As meaningful as the project may be to you, unfortunately it may not be the right time and place for that artist. It doesn't mean don't hold back on going that extra mile to get the song, but don't fall in love with something too much. There are so many good choices for sourcing music and we are confident the right song is out there.

As music supervisor Barry Cole nicely paraphrased, "If a director can't get a song, the audience won't know it." So true! Select another song. There are millions to choose from and millions more where they came from. Music surrounds us. It's compelling and fun, and even more fun when the media producer connects with the right piece and the artist gains exposure. *Kaboom!* A marriage made in heaven.

GLOSSARY

Ancillary income Income generated by a company for services outside its core business or primary product offering.

Approval right The agent, publisher or label representing the songwriter or artist must seek their content prior to licensing the music. This consent is the approval right.

Ask A request for a particular genre, style or mood of a song.

Below-the-line A film production term that centers on the 'line' in 'below-the-line': a separation between the actors, director, producers, and writers from the rest of the crew.

Blanket license A license used to give blanket permission to use any music from a specific catalog. This license is used in a situation where issuing individual music licenses for each piece or each use would be cumbersome. The licensing fees collected from blanket licenses go to pay songwriters and publishers.

Cease-and-desist letter A letter from a lawyer which puts an infringer on notice prior to any action, and usually contains a demand that a certain action be taken.

Clearance, clearing, copyright clearance The process of granting or obtaining permission to use music in a production.

Compilation album The assembly of a variety of songs from various sources to create one album.

Copyright A legal right created by the law that grants the creator of an original work exclusive rights for its use and distribution.

Copyright infringement This occurs when someone violates the exclusive rights of the copyright owner, or essentially uses the song without permission.

Copyright law Part of the laws of the United States that protect intellectual property, including songs, writings and films.

Copyright splits The percentage designated to each writer of a song so that the total amounts to 100%.

Corporate use The use of music in a video or live event by a corporate client and/or its employees.

Cover song When a singer, other than the original recording artist of a song, rerecords his/her own version.

Creative Commons A copyright license that enables the free distribution of an otherwise copyrighted work. A CC license is used when an author wants to give people the right to share, use and build upon a work that they have created.

Cue A singular piece of music use in a program.

Cue sheet A document which is filed with the performing rights societies and contains a detailed listing of each piece of music used in a film or television production in the order that it is heard in the production. The document includes song titles, writer and publisher information, song durations and use types. It is a delivery requirement of all public broadcasters and exhibitors so as to compensate songwriters for the public performance of their music.

Denial When a rights holder disallows use or says no to a music licensing request.

Digital platform Any platform where users can access digital audio and/or audio-visual content.

Exclusivity When one company represents a catalog of music exclusively or when a licensing deal is only allowing the use of a song to a company for a select period of time exclusively. For example, if a song is licensed to an airline company, no other airline company can use the same song for the term of the initial license.

Fair use A legal doctrine that states that some portions of copyrighted materials may be used without permission of the copyright owner, and that not all copying of copyrighted material is a violation of the law, provided the use is fair and reasonable.

Indemnity A promise to defend one in court against a third-party lawsuit.

Initial rights Rights granted for the media requested by a filmmaker based on the expected media of distribution of a film, such as initial film festival rights.

Intranet A company or organization's private secured network.

Jingle Mainly used in advertising: a short slogan, verse or tune designed to be catchy and memorable.

License When an individual or company grants permission to use a piece of music in your production they draw up a license, or agreement, that states the terms of the use. A license is essentially an agreement, on paper, that states how, where, when and for what fee a user is allowed to use the piece of art or, in this case, music.

Licensee The person being granted the music license; hence, a production company or entity.

Licensor The entity granting the license, or permission, for use of the music in a particular territory and term.

Master This refers to a particular recording of a song. The term derives from the physical tape that was used to create a recording; hence, the 'master' tape is the original recording.

Master use license The process of seeking permission from a label (or artist, if the artist is unsigned) to use a master recording in an audio-visual production.

Mechanical license This license grants the user of music the right to reproduce a song in a physical—LP or CD—or digital format, provided the music has already been commercially released in the United States by the copyright owner. This is strictly for the audio reproduction of a song. No visual component is involved.

Metadata Information on a single track that includes the writer(s) name(s), publishing company and the percentage of ownership splits of the writers.

MFN (Most favored nations) When one copyright holder receives the same compensation as another.

Mnemonic In music, a pattern of notes or lyrics used to assist in remembering something, like a brand.

Music rights clearance The process of obtaining permission to use music in a production.

Music supervisor A qualified professional who oversees all music-related aspects of film, television, advertising, video games and other existing or emerging visual media platforms as required.

One-stop shop The user can obtain permission or clearance of both sides of the song at one company, rather than through a number of people.

Opinion letter A letter usually written by a lawyer that gives advice based on the lawyer's special knowledge and understanding of the law as it applies to a particular case. Opinion letters are usually drafted at a client's request.

Option rights Rights that are requested with the initial rights, but are exercisable if and when you need them at a later date.

Performing rights organization or **PRO** An organization that collects and distributes performance royalties on behalf of writers and publishers (e.g., ASCAP, BMI or SESAC). They are essentially royalty collection agencies.

Poor man's copyright Instead of properly registering your composition or work of art with the U.S. Copyright Office, you place the song in an envelope and mail it to yourself. When it is returned to you it has your name and a date stamp to positively prove that the work at least belonged to you as of the date on the stamp. The problem is, there is nothing in the law that acknowledges the validity or accuracy of this method.

Pre-roll The short video ads that appear online before a user's selected content plays.

Production music library Stock or library music that is licensed to film, television, ads and other media clients. Pricing is available through a rate card sheet and both the publishing and recording rights are included for ease of licensing.

Public Broadcasting Service (PBS) A non-profit organization that brings television programming to public television stations in the United States.

Public domain When no one can find any law that gives the legal claim to that property or work, or song. The original owner or creator's rights have expired and anyone can use the music without permission.

Public performance license This license grants permission for music to be heard in public spaces, such as on the radio or television, via on-hold music or in an elevator, hair salon, local bar or other places of work, or even a public website. This license is secured by public broadcasters—say, a radio station or television network—or a business establishment where music is heard.

Publisher A company or entity that represents a catalog of songs or compositions by as few as one person to as many as thousands of writers. Its main objective is to protect and exploit the compositions and collect income for its song catalog's various uses.

Quitclaim deed A quitclaim deed is a release, by the grantor or conveyor of the deed, of any interest in the property described in the deed. Generally, a quitclaim deed relieves the grantor of liability regarding the ownership of the property.

Reuse fees Additional royalty fees paid to musicians, singers or vocalists used on the recording session through their respective unions, such as AFM or SAG-AFTRA.

Re-titling When a catalog representative places a song in a production, and they re-name the song in order to claim a portion of the publishing. This allows the rep to receive back-end income, or royalties, from the public performance of the song he or she placed.

Sides An industry term used to define the publishing or recording of a song. There are two 'sides' to a recorded song, as there are two sides to a coin.

Song pluggers or **reps** Individuals who represent a select catalog and/or artists.

Soundtrack album Generally a CD or digital download release of the songs heard within a film or 'inspired by' the film.

Split dispute Wherein the total ownership value in and to a composition adds up to less than or greater than 100%.

Statutory damages An award of damages granted by a court when a copyright owner's work has been infringed but the owner cannot prove the actual losses he suffered, or the losses are too small to determine.

Step deals These deals allow for a conservative upfront fee, and then monetary bumps, or 'steps,' at different milestones.

Synchronization license This license grants permission to use a song which is locked to a moving image or other audio-visual body of work.

Term The period needed to license a song for a production.

Territory The territory where the production needs to license the music. This generally reflects the regional laws to which the license is subject.

Third-party licensing Exploitation of a recording that pertains to any money received by a label that is generated by not selling music.

Video-on-demand Systems that allow users to access general entertainment content when they choose to, rather than having to watch at a specific broadcast time.

Work-for-hire When an individual is paid a flat fee to complete a project and the work they created becomes the property of the employer. No copyright, if any, is retained by the creator.

Works of authorship A term used in the Copyright Act. Works of authorship include literary, dramatic, musical, artistic and certain other intellectual works.

INDEX

advertising 25–6, 113–24, 135–7; see also trailers/trailer use
agents 144–5
all digital media 100
All.I.Can 51–3
allmusic.com 93
All Music Guide 93
all new media 100
all television media 98–9
American Federation of Musicians 73
ancillary income 34, 43
annual license agreements 78–82
approval parties 149
approval rights 15
apps 137–8
Arrival 64–6
art-house theatrical exhibition 98
artists 139–46
ASCAP (American Society of Composers, Authors and Publishers) 84, 93

Bacharach, Burt 43
Bandcamp 83
basic cable TV 99
Beal, Jeff 68
Beatport 83
Bein, Chuck 114, 116, 119, 120
below-the-line jobs 48, 63
Berne Convention for the Protection of Literary and Artistic Works 9–10
blanket licenses 11, 76, 77–8
Blu-Ray 99
BMI (Broadcast Music Incorporated) 84, 93
Boardwalk Empire 58–9
brand personality, identity and recognition 111–24
Bratt, Peter 55
broad rights 105
Brown, James 55
Bruckheimer, Jerry 41
'bump'/'bumper' music 76
bundling 76
Butch Cassidy and the Sundance Kid 43

cable TV rights 105
Calamar, Gary 53
Callif, Lisa 23–4, 25
Cash, Johnny 2
catalog reps 140
cease-and-desist letters 20–1, 29, 118

clearance: information needed for 96–101; overview of 87–92; overview of music rights 12–14; research tools for 92–4; role of 1–2; sample request for 89–92; *see also* cue sheets; music supervisors
Cole, Barry 53–5, 150
collecting on the back-end 67–8
Columbia Special Products 35
Comeau, Andre 85, 140, 141
commercial music 82–3
commercial request 143–4
compilation albums 34, 45–6
composers 62–73, 77, 116–18, 149
copyright: duration of 9–10; fair use and 22–7, 135, 149; history of 9; infringement of 19–22, 30–1, 117–18; Internet and 29–31; overview of law on 7–8; overview of music 12–14; protections of 10–12; public domain and 27–9; publishing 14; purpose of 8–9; registration 7, 19–20; splits and 16–19; symbols for 22
Copyright Act (1976) 9
copyright clearance 1–2
copyright owners/holders: change in 14–15; finding 14–16; identifying 89; multiple 87–8; two sides and 13–14, 33
corporate piece/corporate use 98, 105, 121–2
Corporation of Public Broadcasting (CPB) 108–9
covering songs 115, 122–4
Creative Commons 83
credits in fair use 26–7
cue sheets 26–7, 76, 94–101, 109
Cutler, Miriam 62, 63, 66–9

David, Hal 43
deal memo documents 69
denials 51–3, 96
Diamond, Neil 2
digital download 100
digital gaming licenses 137–8
digital marketing and advertising 135–7
digital media 100, 101, 105, 119–20, 125–38; *see also* streaming
Digital Millennium Copyright Act (DMCA) 30
digital platforms 125–38
digital search engine platforms 85
digital technology, impact of 3
discovery 83–6
documentaries: challenges and 58–9; composers and 63, 69; denials and 1–2, 51, 96; digital distribution and 130; fair use and 23–4, 25, 149; fees and 129; labels' catalogs and 149; MFN and 107; options and 101; pricing and 55; step deals and 105
documentation, importance of 89
Dolores 55
downloads: annual license agreements and 78, 80; cue sheets and 76; exclusion of 99, 100, 105; mechanical license/fee and 11, 33–4; metadata and 142; music libraries and 77; options and 102; rights for 100, 105, 128, 129; soundtracks and 55; step deals and 132; videograms and 100; VOD services and 130
DVD 99

educational exhibition 98
exclusivity deals 82, 114

fair use 22–7, 135, 149
film festival exhibition/rights 98, 104
film request 144
free on demand (FOD) 129
free TV 99
Fukuyama, Bob 35, 37, 39–40, 41

games 137–8
Garfield, Harry 39
Goldberg, Ron 77
Guild of Music Supervisors 49

harryfox.com 93
home video 99

IMDB.com 94
imprints 44
in-context trailer use 100
indemnity 92, 117–18
independent labels 46
initial rights 101–3
international copyright protection 9–10
Internet 29–31
Internet downloads *see* downloads
Internet Movie Database 94
Internet streaming *see* digital media; streaming
Intranet 136–7
iTunes 142

James Bond films 42
jingles 115–18
Jóhannsson, Jóhann 63–6, 67, 69–70
Johnson, Lyndon 108

Kapp, David 37
Kapp, Mickey 35, 37–9
Keach, James 56–7
K-Tel 37

La Barbara, Joan 65–6
labeling 141–2
labels, record 34–5, 39, 46
lawyers 149
Led Zeppelin 53
Lessig, Lawrence 83
Leviton, Mark 35
licenses: annual 78–82; blanket 11, 76, 77–8; digital gaming 137–8; mechanical 11, 33–4; public performance 11; purpose of 8; synchronization 37–40; synchronization 112; types of 11–12
licensors, point of view of 4
limited theatrical exhibition 98

Mann, Michael 39
master copyright 12–14
master use licensing 34–5
Matson, Andrew 112
MCA Special Markets 41
mechanical license 11, 33–4
mechanical royalties 33–4
media 97–101
media descriptions 91–2
media spread 4
metadata 141–2
MFN (most favored nations) 91, 106–8
Miami Vice 39
mnemonics 115, 116
Mossap, David 51
Motion Picture Information Service (MPIS) 29
motion picture theatrical exhibition 98
'Mozart effect' 112–13
MP3 files 142
music: finding 61–86; overview of copyright for 12–14; role of 1; *see also* composers

music composition agreement 70–3
musicians, union versus non-union 73, 117
music rights clearance 8
music supervisors 47–60, 83, 139–40
music videos 41

National Public Radio (NPR) 109
negotiators, role of 2
new media 100
Nine Inch Nails 51–3
non-exclusivity 114
non-theatrical exhibition 98
non-union musicians 73, 117

one-stop shops 14, 149
opening and closing credits 107
opinion letters 23
options 101–3, 105, 131–2
out-of-context trailer use 101

pay/pay-per-view 99
pdinfo.com 29, 94
penalty fees 118
performance royalties 84
performing rights organizations 67–8, 84
permissions, overview of 2–3
placement companies 144–5
plagiarism 117–18
playlists, retail 111–13
podcasting 99, 100
poor man's copyright 19
Porter, Todd 61–2, 113, 119, 120, 123
Poster, Randall 58–9, 140
pre-roll piece 136, 137
price/pricing 3–4, 103–5; *see also* MFN (most favored nations)
Prisoners 64

production music libraries 73–82
promos 25
Public Broadcasting Act 108
Public Broadcasting Service (PBS) 108–9
public domain 27–9
public performance license 11
public television 108–9
publishers 12–14, 33
publishing copyright 14
publishing rights 68, 69

quitclaim deed 59–60

Radha Krishna Temple 59
"Raindrops Keep Fallin' on My Head" 43
rate cards 74–6, 85
record clubs 35–7
record labels 34–5, 39, 46
requests, examples of 143–4
re-recording songs 122–4
research tools 92–4
retail playlists 111–13
re-titling 145
reuse fees 24–5, 73, 117
reversals 51–3, 55
rights, process of securing 87–109
Roll Bounce 53–5
Rowland, Tom 41
royalties 33–4, 67–8, 84

Savada, Elias 29
SESAC (Society of European Stage Authors and Composers) 84, 93
Sicario 64
sides 13–14
Simpson, Don 41
social media 135
Sokoler, Ben 141, 142
song placement 118–22, 139–46

song pluggers 85
song reps 140
songwriting credit 14
Sony Music 44
SoundCloud 83, 142
soundtracks 40, 41–2, 55–6
split disputes 18–19
splits 16–19
statutory damages 19–20
step deals 105–6, 132–3
streaming 67–8, 100, 105, 119–20, 126, 128–30; *see also* digital media
student films 126, 127–8
subscription TV 99
Summer, Donna 53–5
synchronization license 12, 37–40
synchronization use fees 34–5

television: all media for 98–9; cable 99, 105; free 99; public 108–9; subscription 99
term 3, 97
territory 3, 97
theatrical rights 98, 101, 105
third-party licensing 34–5
Thomas, B.J. 43
Top Gun 41–2
trailer spec 143

trailers/trailer use 25, 100–1; *see also* advertising
True Blood 53

union musicians 73, 117
union reuse fees 24–5
Universal 41
Universal Music 43–4
U.S. Copyright Office 7
use 97
user-generated content 133

video games 137–8
videogram(s) 99–100
video-on-demand (VOD) 99, 119–20, 129, 130–1
videos, music 41
Villeneuve, Denis 63–4
Vimeo 126, 127

Warner Music Group 44
Warner Special Products (WSP) 35, 37–41
WAV files 142
wireless/mobile rights 128
works-for-hire 67
works of authorship 9

YouTube 83, 126–8, 133–5, 142

 Taylor & Francis eBooks

Helping you to choose the right eBooks for your Library

Add Routledge titles to your library's digital collection today. Taylor and Francis ebooks contains over 50,000 titles in the Humanities, Social Sciences, Behavioural Sciences, Built Environment and Law.

Choose from a range of subject packages or create your own!

Benefits for you
- » Free MARC records
- » COUNTER-compliant usage statistics
- » Flexible purchase and pricing options
- » All titles DRM-free.

REQUEST YOUR **FREE** INSTITUTIONAL TRIAL TODAY
Free Trials Available
We offer free trials to qualifying academic, corporate and government customers.

Benefits for your user
- » Off-site, anytime access via Athens or referring URL
- » Print or copy pages or chapters
- » Full content search
- » Bookmark, highlight and annotate text
- » Access to thousands of pages of quality research at the click of a button.

eCollections – Choose from over 30 subject eCollections, including:

Archaeology	Language Learning
Architecture	Law
Asian Studies	Literature
Business & Management	Media & Communication
Classical Studies	Middle East Studies
Construction	Music
Creative & Media Arts	Philosophy
Criminology & Criminal Justice	Planning
Economics	Politics
Education	Psychology & Mental Health
Energy	Religion
Engineering	Security
English Language & Linguistics	Social Work
Environment & Sustainability	Sociology
Geography	Sport
Health Studies	Theatre & Performance
History	Tourism, Hospitality & Events

For more information, pricing enquiries or to order a free trial, please contact your local sales team:
www.tandfebooks.com/page/sales

 Routledge
Taylor & Francis Group

The home of Routledge books

www.tandfebooks.com

Made in the USA
Monee, IL
16 March 2020